LAST WORDS
DYING IN THE OLD WEST

Garry Radison

EAKIN PRESS ⚏ Austin, Texas

FIRST EDITION
Copyright © 2002
By Garry Radison
Published in the United States of America
By Eakin Press
A Division of Sunbelt Media, Inc.
P.O. Drawer 90159 ⬕ Austin, Texas 78709-0159
email: sales@eakinpress.com
⬚ website: www.eakinpress.com ⬚
ALL RIGHTS RESERVED.

1   2   3   4   5   6   7   8   9
1-57168-510-3

Library of Congress Cataloging-in-Publication Data

Radison, Garry
    Last words : dying in the Old West / Garry Radison.– 1st ed.
      p.   cm.
    Includes bibliographical references and index.
    ISBN 1-57168-510-3
    1. Pioneers–West (U.S.)–Death–History–Sources. 2. Outlaws–West
(U.S.)–Death–History–Sources. 3. Pioneers–West (U.S.)–Quotations. 4.
Outlaws–West (U.S.)–Quotations. 5. Last words. 6. Death–Quotations,
maxims, etc. 7. Frontier and pioneer life–West (U.S.)–Sources. 8.
West (U.S.)–History–Sources. 9. West (U.S.)–Biography. I. Title
F596 .R13   2002
978–dc21   2001006854

For Elmer D. McInnes
who continues to search
for the last word.

CONTENTS

INTRODUCTION

From our point of view at the beginning of the twenty-first century, the circumstances of the nineteenth century in western North America were often extraordinary. Indian attacks, lynch mobs, and an armed populace created dramatic death scenes in which even the most humble victim could become significant, his final words remembered for their honesty, courage, vindictiveness, or humor.

Everyone likes a good ending. The Old West provided the setting for many good endings. Cattle towns; mining camps; the permanent gallows at Fort Smith, Arkansas; Indian villages; the camps of buffalo hunters—in such places death was never far away and almost never private. A dying man had an audience and sometimes, at a hanging, for instance, his death was an occasion enjoyed by the assembly. Public hangings, shootouts in the street or in a crowded saloon, public death by misadventure—the community was there and, despite such callous attitudes as "a man every day for breakfast," the community took note, for death has ever been a noteworthy affair.

Legal hangings were often performed in public. Normal activity stopped so that the community, even schoolchildren, could attend. From the neighboring countryside, whole families, lunches packed as for a church picnic, arrived in town and took up their vantage points, eager not to miss a once-in-a-lifetime event. Death had come to town, stirring up curiosity and interest. The spectators took their places, watched, and listened.

As in all ages, a person's character is often revealed in his last moments. But in the Old West, a person's character often brought him to his end. Carrying a revolver was common enough, but using one distinguished a man from other men. A man's reputation could also be his death sentence. And even without a reputation, a person seeking excitement often found, after a roar of confusion, that he was the star of the show, a ring of rowdy spectators suddenly grown silent as they listened for his last words.

The dying were storytellers. A good ending made for a good story. Did he really say that? Or were his words altered to make the story even better? Many last words are documented in newspapers, court records, and coroners' reports. Others are not so well documented. At this late date there is no way of verifying them, but we accept as authentic those words that have had a long oral life. Some of these individuals would be totally forgotten were it not for the good stories associated with their deaths.

But, of course, death has an interest all its own. At the public hanging of a shallow murderer, a nondescript man of no social consequence, a witness noted that "standing in the shadow of death he was invested with a strange dignity." Such a witness would have been waiting for the last words, would perhaps have bestowed on those words a significance that even the speaker was unaware of. And such a witness might have gone home to ponder his own destiny and whether he would be worthy of the "strange dignity" that death brings.

But you may be confident that there were other witnesses who perceived no such dignity, who saw only a miserable nuisance that had to be disposed of. Endicott Peabody, a minister who was in Tombstone when Morgan Earp was shot, saw no such dignity in Earp's ending. In a letter, Peabody said, "We had an excitement on Saturday night. One of the Earps, a family conspicuous for their fighting qualities, was shot in the back while playing billiards in a saloon on the main street. The poor fellow was not killed immediately & suffered frightfully but never uttered a groan. His last sentence was, 'Well, Jim, that's the last game I will ever play.' Fancy a man saying such a thing at such a time. It may seem a certain daring but it argues a sad want of any kind of religious feeling or unsaid human feeling for his wife & family who are in California." Do we judge a man on his last words? Another person might hear in Earp's words the acceptance of death and the poignant sense of loss that is always associated with premature death, the "last game" including all that he ever loved.

Frivolous or not, last words provide the rest of us, the spectators as it were, with a focus. The risk of a meaningless death was never greater than in the Old West. How do we find the humanity in this stranger, a man with little or no past and only rumors of accomplishments? Let him speak; let him, if he will, confess, curse, forgive, regret; let him have whatever human dignity the human voice can conjure.

If the words themselves are often prosaic, the tone still speaks true. There is, in last words, a sincere quality or genuineness that underlies even the most brazen comments. The artificiality of speechmaking or the brigand's bravado cannot completely conceal the quickened heartbeat. The reader may, if he chooses to listen carefully, hear the voice behind the voice: the sense of injustice that expresses itself in profanity, the guilt that attempts to utter a prayer. At such moments we seem to be looking into the dying man's eyes.

Many readers will look for the humor in last words. Some of this humor is deliberate; some unintentional; some fabricated after the fact. H. L. Somerville in "Five Months Term in the Piney Woods" (*Frontier Times*, July 1967), tells the story of an elderly community leader who gathered his children and grandchildren around his deathbed.

> "Got something to tell you," he panted, trying to raise his head. "This name I go by—it isn't really my name. Nor yours, either."
>
> They waited respectfully, wiping away the tears that fell silently down their leathery cheeks.
>
> The old man raised a hand. "Got in trouble in Alabama," he said unsteadily. "I better tell you your real name."
>
> He became silent for a while, as though thinking. One of the younger sons made the mistake of being impatient.
>
> "What is our name, Papa?" he asked with trembling lips.
>
> "Damned if I'll tell you!" the old man snapped stubbornly. "Best not to trust anybody." He turned his face away and died some hours later, still suspicious and silent.

No amount of laughter will destroy his type of dignity. He asks for no sympathy; he wants no understanding. His own man to the end, he chooses silence, perhaps even smiling to himself at his last good joke.

And death is also adept at irony. The people of the Old West were full of expectations that, for many, the suddenness of death left unfulfilled. Often believing they had the upper hand, they were startled at death's swiftness; often unaware of the deadly circumstances shaping up around them, they found their good intentions twisted by a dire irony.

But the ultimate significance of last words is that someone remembered them. Whether found by a researcher a hundred years later, or passed on as folklore, the last words were deemed significant enough to be shared so that we find ourselves bending to hear, as did those original listeners, the gallows officials or bedside relatives. We find ourselves listening for the spirit behind the words, handling them, as it were, like artifacts as we attempt to make them yield something of the final mystery.

Death, after all, comes for each of us. What can one say?

—G. R.

"She was with Mrs. Lee that morning
when the shotguns began to boom
down in the woods. Mrs. Lee
was terribly frightened.
'I know they've killed Bob,' she said.
'You'd better go to him,' advised Miss Pierce.
'If they have shot him,
you might be able to hear
his last words.' "

—C. L. SONNICHSEN
I'll Die Before I'll Run

EXPLORERS AND FUR TRADERS

The first white men to venture into the western half of the North American continent were also the first to document the events that occurred there. From the south came the Spanish; from the north, the fur traders of the Hudson's Bay Company; and between the two were explorers such as Lewis and Clark, and the fur traders of John Jacob Astor. Some of those who stayed in the West became known as Mountain Men, the pathfinders for the thousands of adventurers who would live and die in the West.

MOSES NORTON, Governor
[Prince of Wales' Fort, Rupert's Land, December 29, 1773]

As the tyrannical Hudson's Bay Company governor lay in pain from an intestinal infection, he saw one of his younger Indian wives whispering confidentially with an employee. He rose up in bed and cursed her with his dying breath.

"Goddamn you for a bitch! If I live, I'll knock your brains out!"

CHARLES FLOYD, Sergeant
[Near the future site of Sioux City, Iowa, August 20, 1804]

On the Lewis and Clark expedition up the Missouri River, he fell ill, suffering perhaps from appendicitis.

"I am going away."

MERIWETHER LEWIS, Explorer
[Griner's Stand, Tennessee, October 11, 1809]

Acting somewhat strangely, perhaps depressed, the famous co-leader of the Lewis and Clark Expedition shot himself (or perhaps was murdered) in the middle of the night in a wayside tavern.

"O Lord ... O, Madam, give me some water and heal my wounds ... Take my rifle and finish it for me, my good servant. I am no coward, but I am so strong. It is so hard to die."

GEORGE DROUILLARD, Frontier Scout/Trapper
[Jefferson River, Blackfoot country (Montana), early May, 1810]

Risking attack by Blackfoot warriors, the Lewis and Clark Expedition veteran left camp to hunt, his last words proven untrue only two miles from camp.

"I'm too much of an Indian to be caught by Indians."

JOHN FOX, First Officer
[The mouth of the Columbia River, March 22, 1811]

When John Jacob Astor's ship, the *Tonquin*, arrived at the mouth of the Columbia River, Fox, having been ordered despite bad weather to find a safe passage into the river, disappeared with four men in a longboat into the treacherous seas.

"My uncle was drowned here not many years ago,
and now I am going to lay my bones with his."

JOHN COLTER, Trapper/Frontiersman
[Dundee Reach, near present-day New Haven, Missouri,
late November, 1813]

Friend of Daniel Boone, member of the Lewis and Clark Expedition, the old frontiersman had married a girl from a poor family with no social standing, a "corncracker" who kept a journal in which she recorded his death from yellow jaundice.

"Nancy, I's sorry I ever called ye a corncracker. Ye heerd whut Dan'l Boone said. Ye air as great a lady as any down in St. Louis. Ye tuk care o' me better'n anybody would. Better call in ol' Wah Hoss [an Indian friend] *now, fer I'm goin'."*

MIKE FINK, Boatman
[Near Fort Henry, mouth of the Yellowstone River, early winter, 1822]

Famed Mississippi boatman and troublemaker, Fink, with friends, joined a fur-trading expedition and in a drunken gathering killed his best friend while attempting to shoot a tin cup off his friend's head. Not believing Fink's last words, another friend immediately killed him.

"I didn't mean to! My boy, my boy, I didn't mean to!"

ANTOINE RIVET, Fur Trader/Voyageur
[Fort St. John, Peace River country (British Columbia),
early November, 1823]

Arriving by canoe at the Hudson's Bay post, which was being abandoned and where Indians had recently killed the only remaining white man, Rivet and his crew were fired upon and killed by Indians hidden in the trees.

"Fire, you dogs, but you will never make me afraid!"

EZRA KIND, Prospector
[Black Hills, June 1834]

His last words were found in 1887, scratched on a slab of sandstone now known as the "Thoen Stone."

[On one side]

came to these hills in 1833
seven of us
De Lacompt
Ezra Kind
GW Wood
T Brown
R Kent
Wm King
Indian Crow
all ded but me
Ezra Kind
Killed by Ind beyond the high hill
got our gold June 1834

[On the other side]

Got all of the gold we could carry
our ponys all got by the Indians
I hav lost my gun and nothing to
eat and
indians hunting me

JOHN ROWLAND, Hudson's Bay Factor
[Fort Pitt, Prince Rupert's Land, May 30, 1854]

Hearing that his son was taking a beating outside, the feisty Rowland came running out of the office, threw up his hands, yelled at his son, and immediately died, probably from a heart attack.

"Can't you do better than that?"

4

JOHN McLOUGHLIN, Hudson's Bay Factor
[1857]

After a career with the Hudson's Bay Company, for whom he controlled fur trading and settlement in the Columbia River country in Oregon for more than twenty years, he died quietly in bed, his last words a pun in answer to the question, *"Comment allez-vous?"*

"To God."

TEXAS INDEPENDENCE

As the rapidly growing non-Mexican population of Texas began to dominate Texas politics, the movement toward independence from Mexico caught fire. In the memorable battles of the Alamo and Goliad, the slaughtered Texans provided models of courage for their countrymen, who finally made the dream of independence a reality in the battle at San Jacinto, where the Mexican army, led by Santa Anna, was defeated.

MOSES AUSTIN, Colonizer
[Potosi, Missouri, June 10, 1821]

In the midst of preparations to implement his dream of a colony in Texas, he caught pneumonia, his last words, paraphrased by his wife in a letter, passing the dream on to his son, Stephen Austin.

> *"He called me to his bedside and with much distress and difficulty of speech he begged me to tell you to take his place, and if god in his wisdom thought best to disappoint him in the accomplishment of his plans formed for the benefit of the family, he prayed him to extend his goodness to you and to enable you to go on with the business in the same way he would have done."*

ISAAC MILLSAPS, Alamo Defender
[The Alamo, San Antonio, Texas, March 3, 1836]

Three days before the battle, he wrote a letter to his wife.

My dear, dear ones

We are in the fortress of the Alamo a ruined Church that has most fell down. The Mexicans are here in large numbers they have kept up a constant fire since we got here. All of our boys are well & Capt. Martin is in good spirits. Early this morning I watched the Mexicans drilling just out of range they was marching up and down with such order. They have bright red & blue uniforms and many canons. Some here at this place believe that the main army has not come up yet. I think they is all here even Santana. Col. Bowie is down sick and had to be to bed I saw him yesterday & he is still ready to fight. He didn't know me from last spring but did remember Wash. He tells all that help will be here soon & it makes us feel good. We have beef & corn to eat but no coffee, bag I had fell off on the way here so it was all spilt. I have not see Travis but 2 times since here he told us all this morning that Fanning was going to be here early with many men and there would be a good fight. He stays on the wall some but mostly to his room. I hope help comes soon cause we cant fight them all. Some says he is going to talk some tonight & group us better for defense. If we fail here get to the river with the children all Texas will be before the enemy we get so little news here we know nothing. There is no discontent in our boys some are tired from loss of sleep or a rest. The mexicans are shooting every few minutes but most of the shots fall inside & do no harm. I don't know what else to say they is calling for all letters, kiss the dear children for me and believe as I do that all will be well & God protects us all.

Isaac

If any men come through there tell them to hurry with powder for it is short I hope you get this & know—I love you all.

WILLIAM BARRET TRAVIS, Lieutenant Colonel
[The Alamo, San Antonio, Texas, March 6, 1836]

Knowing his force was badly outnumbered by Santa Anna's Mexican army, he and his 136 men had resolved to fight to the death.

"The Mexicans are upon us—give 'em Hell!"

ALMERON DICKERSON, Alamo Defender
[The Alamo, San Antonio, Texas, March 6, 1836]

In the midst of the fighting, he took a moment to run to his wife, Susannah, before going back out to face the enemy.

"Great God, Sue, the Mexicans are inside our walls!
If they spare you, save my child!"

EIGENAUER, Texas Defender
[Goliad, Texas, March 19, 1836]

One of many defenders of German origin, he fought in Colonel Fannin's desperate defeat by the Mexican army and died on the battlefield, whispering his last words to his friend Hermann Ehrenberg.

"Ich starb für Texas." [I died for Texas.]

MANUEL FERNANDEZ CASTRILLON, Mexican General
[San Jacinto, Texas, April 21, 1836]

As his soldiers fled before the furious Texans at the decisive battle for Texas independence, he stood his ground.

[In Spanish]
"I've been in forty battles and never showed my back.
I'm too old to do it now!"

ANONYMOUS MEXICAN DRUMMER BOY
[San Jacinto, Texas, April 21, 1836]

Both legs broken, unable to retreat with his comrades, he futilely begged for his life.

"Ave Maria purisima! Per Dios, salva me vida!"
[Hail Mary most pure! For God, save my life!]

ANONYMOUS MEXICAN SOLDIER
[San Jacinto, Texas, April 21, 1836]

Like many of his fellows who possibly had no hand in the killing of Texans at Goliad and the Alamo, he tried to surrender but was shot down without mercy by the enraged Texans, who charged screaming, "Remember the Alamo! Remember Goliad!"

"Me no Alamo! Me no Goliad!"

STEPHEN F. AUSTIN, Texas Secretary of State
[Texas, December 27, 1836]

Only forty-three years old, the "father of Texas" died after catching a severe chill, his final thoughts of Texas more wishful thinking than fact.

"Texas is recognized! Did you see it in the papers?"

SAMUEL HOUSTON
[Huntsville, Texas, July 26, 1863]

The former war hero, governor, congressman, and president of the Republic of Texas, died in bed of pneumonia with his wife at his bedside.

"Texas—Texas!—Margaret!"

JOHN COFFEE "JACK" HAYES

[Near Oakland, California, April 21, 1866]

Best known as a Texas Ranger and soldier, he died quietly at his home, remembering the glory of the birth of Texas.

"It's San Jacinto Day!"

FEUDS AND DUELS

In parts of the West, feuding between families or rival business interests such as cattlemen often resulted in violence. Long-lived feuds in Texas and Arkansas claimed many lives. A code of honor played a role in the feuds, the same code that prompted many individuals to enact their own private and short-lived feuds on the dueling field. Though many of the feuds were a struggle for wealth, some men felt the need to uphold their honor, knowing that it was just as dangerous to walk away from a fight as it was to meet the challenge. Pride, arrogance, misplaced good will, and a certain amount of naivete were the downfall of many of them.

JOSHUA COTTON
[Livingston, Mississippi, June 1835]

A member of the Mystic Clan, an organization dedicated to slave revolt, he was implicated in a plot to instigate a slave uprising and was lynched. With his last words, he intimated that the Mystic Clan would seek revenge on the crowd.

"Take care of yourselves tonight and tomorrow night!"

WILLIAM REDD, Captain
[San Antonio, Texas, c. summer 1840]

Insulted for his lack of action during an Indian scare, Redd found himself in a duel with Major Wells. Though duel participants, more interested in honor than death, often aimed to miss, Redd made it clear that he was serious.

"I aim for your heart."

JOSEPH GOODBREAD
[Shelbyville, Texas, summer 1840]

Lounging in front of a store, unarmed, he was taken by surprise by well-armed Charley Jackson, to whom he had written a threatening letter.

"I didn't mean to do any more than scare you a little, Charley."

SQUIRE HUMPHREYS
[Shelbyville, Texas, October 19, 1841]

Accused of complicity in the killing of Charley Jackson, he was found guilty at a mass-meeting trial by the folks of Shelbyville and taken to a hanging tree by his enemies, among whom was Watt Moorman.

"I was after you too, Watt. You thrashed me with a hickory stick, and now instead of killing you, you are going to hang me. So be at it. Let the thing be over and done with."

WILLIAM MCFADDEN
[Shelbyville, Texas, October 19, 1841]

Wounded in the leg during his capture, he cursed the same angry folk of Shelbyville, who were preparing to hang him in the Old West tradition of slapping the horse out from under him.

"You have stolen my life, and you'll wade through blood for it. You fellows that are grinning now will bleed and die to pay for this murder. ...Oh, damn you, you ain't worth killing. Here, help me up on this horse."

GEORGE DIBBLE, Miner
[Industry Bar, California, November 1, 1851]

He underestimated the effect of the bullet he received in the chest during a formal duel with a gambler who had a faulty sense of honor.

*"You son of a bitch! You fired before the word.
You have nearly killed me!"*

ALEXANDER MCCLANAHAN
[Grass Valley, California, February 21, 1857]

Having insulted Francis Van Moore, who challenged him, McClanahan armed himself, and in a close encounter both men fired. Van Moore, not fatally wounded, fell in the darkened room, and McClanahan hastily left with two friends. Perhaps unaware that he was shot, he enjoyed his triumph for only a moment, then collapsed in the street.

"I shot his damn head off."
[Collapses] *"My God! I am gone!"*

DAVID COLBRETH BRODERICK, Senator
[Fort Mason, San Fransciso, California, September 16, 1859]

Mortally wounded in a duel with former California Supreme Court Justice David S. Terry on September 13, Broderick was taken to a friend's home, where, four days later, he died. On his deathbed he said,

> *"The killed me because I was opposed to the extension of slavery and the corruption of justice."*

Close to death, he uttered,

> *"I die; protect my honor."*

FRANK KING, Rancher
[Los Angeles, California, July 6, 1865]

Having been threatened, along with his brothers, by rancher Robert Carlisle, King accosted Carlisle in a bar. Both men were killed in the shootout.

> *"I don't care for your mouth, Carlisle, and I especially don't care for you!"*

MARION MORE, Mine Owner
[Near Silver City, Idaho, 1868]

Still smarting from a reluctant agreement with neighboring mine owners who were encroaching on More's mine, he was returning to his hotel after a banquet when he chanced upon two gunmen hired by his opposition. In the ensuing argument, he was shot.

"They have stolen the mine and now their man . . . has killed me."

DAVE FREAM, Cowboy
[Near Thrall, Texas, spring 1870]

Approached on the range by rancher and rustler-killer Print Olive, who wanted to know if Fream had shot at Olive's brother several days prior, he replied, a bit too slow, with a revolver.

"No, but I'd damn well like to take a pop at you!"

EDGAR YEAGER
[Walkerville, Texas, October 12, 1869]

When John Vinyard accused eighteen-year-old Yeager of stating that another man was better than Vinyard, Yeager's smooth reply aroused Vinyard's homicidal nature.

"I didn't say so. I said I wouldn't be surprised if he was."
[Gunshot] *"Murder!"*

BILLIE WILSON, Cowboy
[On the Goodnight-Loving Trail, New Mexico, late October, 1871]

Whiskey-talk after a hard day on the trail led Billie to brag of his fighting abilities to another cowboy who, thinking he was being insulted, made an equivalent boast, which prompted Billie to draw a knife.

" 'Star weno!" [*Esta Bueno:* It is good.]

SAMUEL BESSE, Rancher
[Near Little Lake, California, February 1, 1872]

Living near his own property in a house owned by his in-laws, with whom he was quarreling, he refused to be evicted and drew a knife.

"I'll hold all the law will allow me to!"

DAN FIELDER, Homesteader
[Near Caldwell, Kansas, April 1, 1872]

In a neighbor's dugout, gun ready (he got off the first shot), he responded to the challenge of McCarty, whom Fielder had previously beaten up.

"Here I am. Come in here if you want anything."

WILLIAMS, Settler
[San Saba County, Texas, February 1, 1873]

When a horse race and drinking bout turned violent, he was first shot, then attacked by his adversary who, literally, had an ax to grind.

"For God's sake, Jackson, don't kill me with the ax!"

GABRIEL SLAUGHTER, Rancher
[Indianola, Texas, March 11, 1874]

Aboard the *Clinton,* in conversation with his friend Bill Sutton as they waited to sail, he noticed two of Bill's enemies approaching.

"Here comes Jim and Billy. Hadn't we better get our guns?"

WILLIAM SUTTON, Rancher
[Indianola, Texas, March 11, 1874]

One of the main participants in the Taylor-Sutton feud, he responded to Gabriel Slaughter's question concerning the approach of two Taylors aboard the *Clinton.*

"No, don't worry. They are too much men to do anything now."

TIM WILLIAMSON, Ranch Foreman
[Near Mason, Texas, May 1875]

After having reluctantly consented to go to town with his enemy Sheriff Clark, he lay wounded on the road, bushwhacked by possible Clark conspirators, one of whom he recognized.

"Pete, this is all foolishness. I've got a family and you've got a family. Let's stop it now."

JOHN WOHRLE, Ex-Deputy Sheriff
[Mason, Texas, August 10, 1875]

Having been involved in the death of Tim Williamson, Wohrle was helping dig a well when he was casually approached by Williamson's good friend Scott Cooley, who shot Wohrle in the head after he had asked Wohrle why he had shot Williamson.

"Because I had to!"

NELSON "COONEY" MITCHELL, Rancher
[Granbury, Texas, October 9, 1875]

With the noose around his neck, having been found guilty (on Jim Truitt's testimony) of murdering two of Truitt's brothers and wounding Jim Truitt, he addressed his accuser, who remained silent after each question.

"Jim, when you didn't have nothing but one pony and a wagon, didn't I take you in and feed you? Didn't I? When you wanted to go to preaching, didn't I buy you the first suit of clothes you ever had? Didn't I buy you a Bible—a good Bible—to start you out?"

JOE BRISCOE, Buffalo Hunter
[Near Fort Griffin, Texas, November 1876]

Responding to an insult by fellow buffalo hunter Pat Garrett, the ax-wielding Briscoe was shot by Garrett, who later felt remorse when Briscoe apologized.

"Won't you come over here and forgive me?"

TOM LUMPKINS, Buffalo Hunter
[Rath City, Texas, early April, 1877]

Uninterested in killing Indians, he belittled the Indian-hating hidemen, finally wounding one hunter, whose friend took up the battle with Lumpkins.

"Get out of the way, Crawford; he has insulted me!"

FRED SMITH, Rancher
[Near Thrall, Texas, early September, 1876]

Trying to quietly leave Texas, he was intercepted and challenged by Print Olive over a night attack in which Olive's brother was killed.

*"I don't want to fight you, Print. I just want
to leave the country, peaceful-like."*

W. R. HENRY, Captain
[San Antonio, Texas, April 8, 1862]

Angry, perhaps drunk, Henry picked a fight with a reluctant Captain Adams, who shot him.

*"God damn you, I will put two six shooter bullets
through your brain anyhow!"*

GEORGE BRASSELL
[Shiloh, Texas, September 20, 1876]

Caught up in the animosities of the Taylor-Sutton feud, he and his father were taken from their home and shot by a mob of masked men.

> *"If you're going to kill us, kill us all. And you might as well do it here and now, because I am not going any farther. You can take me to court if you want to, but you can't prove anything because I haven't done anything."*

ROBERT OLIVE, Rancher
[Near Plum Creek, Nebraska, December 1, 1878]

Wounded while attempting to arrest rustlers, he lingered several days, long enough for his wife, Mink, and brother, Print, to be with him.

> *"Tell mother I heard her prayer—but it was no use....
> That's all, Mink honey. Take care of our baby ... I only wanted to be like you, Print."*

AMI KETCHUM, Settler
[Near Plum Creek, Nebraska, December 11, 1878]

Suspected of rustling, and having been involved in the fight in which Bob Olive was mortally wounded, he and Luther Mitchell refused to cooperate with Print Olive, who first offered them whiskey, then, frustrated by their silence, lynched them.

"Take your damned liquor and keep it!"

MART FROST, Rancher
[Near Little Lake, California, December 28, 1883]

Many years of bad blood finally erupted in a gunfight when, accusing his two nephews of being the cause of all the trouble, he couldn't stand their denial.

"You are a damned lying son of a bitch!"

M. C. BUCHANAN
[Durango, Colorado, May 23, 1882]

After a small quarrel with George Woods in a saloon, Buchanan, in conversation with someone else, referred to Woods in a voice loud enough to reach Woods who, gun in hand, said he would speak, and then he let his bullets talk for him.

"I had an argument with a man and he won't speak to me."

[Woods: "I'll speak to you!"]

"I haven't got a gun!"

JACK HARRIS, Theater Owner
[San Antonio, Texas, July 11, 1882]

In his theater, he was shot by the renowned gunfighter Ben Thompson, with whom he had an ongoing feud.

"He took advantage of me and shot me from the dark."

JONATHAN DAVIS
[Chouteau, Oklahoma Territory, December 20, 1885]

After having thrown drunk Kit Ross out of his home two years earlier, he was not prepared for the shot in the back when Ross casually passed him in a store.

"Kit, I believe we will have some snow."

SAM SEALS, Cowboy
[Colorado City, Texas, August 19, 1885]

After a night of drinking, he encountered Wade Hudson, another cowboy, with whom he had earlier argued and who now, from behind a horse, wanted to know if Seals was ready to fight.

"Yes, by God, I am. Turn yourself loose! ... If you want to fight me, get away from that horse. I'll fight you, but if you stand behind that horse, you're a coward!"

MART DUGGAN, Ex-Marshal
[Leadville, Colorado, April 9, 1888]

Shot in the back of the head, he refused to cooperate with law officers when they asked for the name of his assailant, although he had named Bailey Youngson when he first regained consciousness.

"I don't know who shot me. Don't know who it was. Was one of the gang. I'll die before I tell you."

[Officer: "Was it Bailey Youngson?"]

"No!"

21

NATHANIEL KINNEY, Vigilante Leader
[Forsyth, Missouri, August 20, 1888]

The leader of the Bald Knobbers, busy at the court's request taking inventory in a store that belonged to an anti-vigilante, was caught off guard by two other anti-vigilantes, who were looking for their chance to kill Kinney and plead self-defense.

> *"I told you not to come in this store while I was in here.*
> *You son of a bitch, I'll kill you!"*

R. E. "BOB" STAFFORD, Rancher
[Columbus, Texas, July 7, 1890]

Having asked a favor and received a promise from "friend" and city marshal Larkin Hope, Stafford later confronted Hope with the broken promise, only to be gunned down by Hope and his brother, who had been looking for an opportunity to kill the Stafford brothers.

> *"Larkin, why didn't you do as you promised me?*
> *I don't think I've been treated right."*

JOHN STAFFORD, Rancher
[Columbus, Texas, July 7, 1890]

Seeing his brother in trouble with City Marshal Larkin Hope, he tried to intervene and was shot by Larkin's brother, Marian. Larkin finished him off before Mrs. Stafford arrived.

> *"Mr. Hope, allow me to take my brother home ... For God's sake, Larkin, don't shoot me again. Marian has already killed me. Let me live 'til my wife gets here. Yonder she comes now."*

PETER DUCHARME
[Near Calgary, Northwest Territories, Canada, June 12, 1896]

Seeking revenge against Charles Godin, who had testified against him months earlier, he ambushed Godin and wounded him fatally, but lost possession of the revolver and was killed by Godin.

"I have been laying for you!"

SAM HOUSTON REESE, Rancher
[Columbus, Texas, March 16, 1899]

Having just come into town on business, he was threatened and then shot by several men, participants in the long-running Townsend-Stafford feud, which took the life of the Stafford brothers in 1890.

"I want no more of this."

"LONG TOM" SEARS, Gambler
[Porterville, California, December 13, 1901]

Going into an alley to settle an old grievance with friend and partner Jim McKinney, he threw aside his revolver.

"All right, Jim, if we can't be friends, shoot me!"

GEORGE RIDDLE
[Spokogee, Indian Territory, September 22, 1902]

Friend of the McFarlands in the McFarland-Brooks feud, the old man, after being slapped by John Brooks, backed out of the post office and came upon his enemy Willis Brooks.

"Brooks, you can kill me; I am unarmed."

WILLIS B. BROOKS, Rancher
[Spokogee, Indian Territory, September 22, 1902]

One of the chief participants in the McFarland-Brooks feud, he replied to George Riddle, shot him, and then was shot down.

"I will kill you!"

HARRISON DEARING, Constable
[El Dorado, Arkansas, October 9, 1902]

Trying to prevent an impending conflict between Marshal Tucker and the Parnell brothers, he was shot down in the ensuing gunfight.

"For God's sake, let's stop this row, Jim ... for God's sake, stop this, boys! Don't have any trouble."

TOM PARNELL
[El Dorado, Arkansas, October 9, 1902]

Apparently influenced by Constable Dearing, he tried to leave the conflict but was twice drawn back by accusations of cowardice, the second accusation goading him into gunplay.

"Tucker, I am going to leave this with you ... I don't want you to think I'm a damn coward because I am walking off from you!"

"BUTTERMILK" BILL HENSLEY
[Denver, Colorado, December 20, 1905]

Holding a twenty-year grudge, he finally cornered and killed millionaire William J. Wilson, then shot himself.

"At last I've got you alone, where I want you! You've gotten away from me before, but you'll not do it this time! Your time has come. Prepare to die!"

WILLIAM J. WILSON, Cattle Baron
[Denver, Colorado, December 20, 1905]

Aware that he was being stalked by his old nemesis Buttermilk Bill, he took four bullets before collapsing and calling for help.

"That gambler is killing me! Take him away. For God's sake, won't someone stop him? ... Tell my brother Andy— and call Dr. Grant—the pain is awful!"

C. L. "GUNPLAY" MAXWELL, Outlaw
[Price, Utah, August 29, 1909]

Burdened with a long-standing grudge, Maxwell, under a pretense of friendship, lured Deputy Johnson to the railroad tracks, then drew, fired, and missed, receiving two slugs in the chest.

"Don't shoot again, Johnson; you have killed me."

JOE ALLEMAND, Sheepherder
[Near Ten Sleep, Wyoming, April 2, 1909]

In the ongoing war between cattlemen and sheepmen, Allemand and two others were shot down in their camp by a gang of anonymous cowboys who ordered them to come out of their sheep wagon.

"It is a hell of a time of the night to come out."

BILL DUNN, Fugitive
[Pawnee, Oklahoma, November 6, 1896]

He confronted lawman Canton, who immediately shot him.

"Frank Canton, goddamn you! I've got it in for you!"

THEODORE GARTEN, Gambler
[Flagstaff, Arizona, spring 1901]

Intoxicated, and angry with Al Simms for paying too much attention to a favorite prostitute, he attacked Simms, beating him over the head with his gun until Simms ripped open Garten's stomach with a hunting knife.

"Joe, you tell the sheriff when he comes that this was all my fault. He is not to arrest Al Simms al all."

ALMA ALBERT "AB" MURDOCK
[Near Heber City, Utah, June 27, 1911]

Suspected of horse theft or dallying with Mrs. Scruggs, Murdock was chased and then ambushed by Alvin Scruggs, who, rifle raised, ordered Murdock to throw up his hands.

"Go to hell!"

THE MEXICAN WAR

EWEN CAMERON, Captain
[Near Mexico City, Mexico, April 26, 1843]

Refusing the blindfold, he was shot by a firing squad for leading an escape attempt after he and his men were captured during a raid into Mexico.

"For the liberty of Texas, Ewen Cameron
can look death in the face! Fire!"

ANONYMOUS CALIFORNIO
[Near Sonoma, California, early July, 1846]

As Fremont's Americans took control of California during the Mexican War, they shot the two nephews of an elderly Californio and then shot him.

"Is it possible that you kill these young men for no reason at all?
It is better that you kill me who am old."

WILLIAM WATSON, Colonel
[Monterrey, Mexico, September 21, 1846]

Attempting to take the city of Monterrey during the Mexican War, he was encouraged to fall back under the heavy fire.

"Never, boys, never will I yield an inch! I have too much Irish blood in me to give up!"

SAMUEL HAMILTON WALKER, Captain
[Huamantla, Mexico, October 9, 1847]

Though always known as a Texas Ranger, the man who helped develop the famous Walker Colt pistol was mortally wounded in battle while serving in the U.S. Dragoons.

"Although your captain has fallen, never surrender, boys."

INDIANS

PUSHMATAHA, Choctaw Chief
[Washington, D.C., December 24, 1824]

While waiting for government decisions concerning his people, he took sick and, shortly before he died, made a request of his visitor, General Andrew Jackson.

"When I am dead, fire the big guns over me."

RED JACKET, Seneca Chief
[Near Buffalo, New York, January 20, 1830]

The elderly chief who had fought for the British during the Revolutionary War and for the Americans during the War of 1812 approached his death with the knowledge that his people and their way of life were dying out.

"I am about to leave you, and when I am gone, and my warnings shall be no longer heard or regarded, the craft and avarice of the white man will prevail. Many winters have I breasted the storm, but I am an aged tree, and can stand no longer. My leaves are fallen, my branches are withered, and I am shaken by every breeze. Soon my aged trunk will be prostrate, and the foot of the exulting foe of the Indian may

29

be placed upon it in safety; for I leave none who will be able to avenge such an indignity. Think not I mourn for myself. I go to join the spirits of my fathers, where age cannot come. But my heart fails when I think of my people who are soon to be scattered and forgotten.

[Dying request] Bury me by the side of my former wife; and let my funeral be according to the customs of our nation. Let me be dressed and equipped as my fathers were, that their spirits may rejoice in my coming. Be sure that my grave be not made by a white man; let them not pursue me there!"

FOUR BEARS, Mandan Warrior
(Fort Clark, near present-day Bismarck,
North Dakota, July 30, 1837)

One of many of his tribe who caught smallpox, shortly before he died he addressed his tribesmen with a speech that was translated and recorded by a white man.

"I have done everything that a red Skin could do for them. And how have they repaid it? With ingratitude! I have never called a white man a dog, but today, I do pronounce them to be a set of black-hearted dogs! They have deceived me! They, whom I always considered as brothers, have turned out to be my worst enemies.

I do not fear death, my friends. You know it! But to die with my face rotten, that even the wolves will shrink with horror at seeing me, and say to themselves, "That is the Four Bears, the friend of the Whites!"

Listen well what I have to say, as it will be the last time you will hear me! Think of your wives, children, brothers, sisters, friends! All that you hold dear are all dead, or dying, with their faces all rotten, caused by those dogs, the whites! Think of all that, my friends, and rise together and not leave one of them alive! The Four Bears will act his part!"

O-TAT-TO-YE, Blackfoot Brave
(Canadian Prairies, c. 1850)

Wounded in a raid on a large Cree encampment, the young warrior could retreat no further, fell to the ground, and asked his friend, Little Bear, to place a cloth over his face and to abandon him to the approaching Cree.

"Take the cloth from my face ... Kiss me ...
Now place the cloth once more;
I would not see them when they come."

CHENOWETH, Cascade Chief
[Bradford Store settlement, Washington Territory, late March, 1856]

Found guilty of participating in the Yakima uprising, he was hanged by simply kicking a barrel out from under him. Because the fall did not break his neck, he managed to speak before a soldier shot him to prevent a slow death by strangulation.

"I am not afraid of the dead."

QUALCHAN, Yakima Warrior
[Latah Creek, Washington Territory, September 24, 1858]

Hanged by the military as an example to the unruly Indians of the Northwest, in his last moments Qualchan, pleading for his life, embarrassed his father, Chief Owhi.

"Stop, friends! Don't kill me! I will give you money and many horses if you will not kill me! Many Indians will be angry!"

ANONYMOUS RESERVE INDIAN
[Brazos Indian Reserve, Texas, May 23, 1859]

As Colonel Baylor led a 250-man militia across the reserve in search of Indians to punish for recent raids, an old man, apparently harmless, approached on a pony and, having made his identification, raised a pistol, attempting to kill the group's leader.

"Howdy do, howdy do." [Pointing] *"Him Captain?"*

WHITE DOG, Sioux Warrior
[Mankato, Minnesota, December 26, 1862]

Hanged in the largest mass execution in U.S. history for his part in the Sioux uprising, he and thirty-seven other warriors, moments before the drop, began shouting their names and the names of friends or relatives.

"White Dog. I'm here! I'm here!"

AH-CHE-WUN, Lamachis Indian
[Victoria, British Columbia, July 4, 1863]

In the years following the gold rush of 1858, Ah-Che-wun, "The Man Who Walked Through Rock," a member of the Lamachis tribe, had sworn to force the white man from Indian lands. Suspected of twenty murders, he eluded capture by hiding in a well hidden cave. Finally captured, he went to the gallows boasting of killing many Americans and Englishmen.

"For eleven Boston and King George I shoot with my arrows, only one Indian pay with his life because he great chief. He worth many men and women, Ah-Che-Wun."

WHITE ANTELOPE, Cheyenne Chief
[Sand Creek, Colorado, November 29, 1864]

Too old to fight, he also refused to retreat, singing his death song when soldiers unexpectedly attacked the friendly Indians of Black Kettle's camp.

"Nothing lives long, except the earth and the mountains."

OO-LATH-LA-HI-NA, Kickapoo Woman
[On Dove Creek, Texas, January 8, 1865]

Having some education at a white man's school, she attempted to prevent an attack by soldiers who apparently did not realize her tribe was friendly with white men.

"I will go out and talk with the white Captain. He thinks we are Comanches. The white men won't shoot a woman."

TWO FACE, Oglala Chief
[Fort Laramie, Wyoming Territory, May 26, 1865]

After returning two white women captives to the safety of Fort Laramie, Two Face and Blackfoot, a Cheyenne subchief, were found guilty of abusing the women and went to the scaffold.

"Meah washita." [I am brave.]

ANONYMOUS OGLALA WARRIOR
[Near Fort Buford, Dakota Territory, November 1868]

Having ambushed mail carrier Yellowstone Kelly, the warrior and Kelly continued to fire at each other, the warrior, before charging on foot, responding to Kelly's shout, "Who are you?"

"Oglala me."

OLD JOSEPH, Nez Perce Chief
[Wallowa Valley, Oregon, 1871]

Dying of natural causes, he passed on the chieftainship to his son, who would become the dignified, courageous Chief Joseph.

"My son, my body is returning to my mother earth, and my spirit is going very soon to see the Great Spirit. When I am gone, think of your country. You are the chief of these people. They look to you to guide them. Always remember that your father never sold his country. You must stop your ears whenever you are asked to sign a treaty selling your home."

SATANK, Kiowa Chief
[Texas, 1871]

Being transported back to Texas to stand trial for murder, he decided to go down fighting, singing his death song just before attacking the guards.

*"O Sun, you remain forever, but we Koitsenko must die.
O Earth, you remain forever, but we Koitsenko must die."*

TEBEKOKECHICKWABE, Chippawa
[Brainerd, Minnesota, July 23, 1872]

Implicated in the murder of a young white woman whose body was never found, he and his brother were taken from jail by a lynch mob. Tebekokechickwabe attempted to save his life by accusing his hanging brother.

"That's the man that killed the girl! Let me go and I will show you where her head is hid away!"

KICKING BIRD, Kiowa Leader
[Fort Sill, Oklahoma, May 4, 1875]

Having avoided war with the whites, he was not exiled to Florida with other Kiowas, who considered him a traitor and who probably poisoned his coffee.

"I am dying. I have taken the white man's hand ... I am not sorry for it. Tell my people to keep in the good path. I am dying holding fast the white man's hand."

CAPTAIN JACK, Modoc Leader
[Fort Klamath, Oregon, October 3, 1873]

Sentenced to hang for leading an uprising in which General Canby was killed, the only general killed in the Indian wars, Captain Jack was told that he would be going to heaven.

"Well, preacher, I tell you what I'll do with you. I will give you twenty-five head of ponies if you will take my place today, as you said it is such a nice place, because I do not like to go right now."

COCHISE, Apache Chief
[Chiricahua Agency, New Mexico, spring 1874]

Seriously ill from a debilitating disease, he spoke with Indian Agent Jeffords about the possibility of them seeing each other again.

"I believe good friends will meet somewhere."

CRAZY HORSE, Oglala Sioux Warrior
[Camp Robinson, Nebraska, September 5, 1877]

Resisting arrest, he was stabbed with a bayonet held by an Indian policeman.

"He has killed me now!"

SITTING BULL, Hunkpapa Medicine Man
[Near Mobridge, South Dakota, December 15, 1890]

After submitting to arrest by the Indian police, Sitting Bull, rebuked by his son, verbally resisted the officers and was shot by Bull Head.

"Then I shall not go."

PASCALE, Kootenais Indian
[Missoula, Montana, December 19, 1890]

He converted to Catholicism before he was hanged in the jail yard along with three other Indians for murdering white men.

"I did wrong. This is good Friday, a great day for everybody.
I bid everybody goodbye."

Cha Nopa Uhah
Chief Two Sticks
[Deadwood, South Dakota, January 4, 1894]

On the scaffold for murder, he sang his death song before two hundred spectators.

"My heart is not bad; I did not kill the cowboys—the Indian boys killed them. I have killed many Indians but never killed a white man. The Great Father and the men under him should talk to me and I would show them that I was innocent ... My heart knows I am not guilty and I am happy."

Almighty Voice, Fugitive
[Near Batoche, Northwest Territories, Canada, May 30, 1897]

After murdering Sergeant Colebrook in 1895, the youthful Cree, killer of three of the six Mounties slain by Indians in the Canadian West, was finally trapped in a wooded area by the North-West Mounted Police and killed at the end of a two-day battle.

*"Brothers, we have fought a good fight. Send me food.
I am starving. Tomorrow we will fight again!"*

Washakie, Shoshoni Chief
[Near Fort Washakie, Wyoming, February 20, 1900]

The ninety-year-old chief, having led his people in a long and enduring peace with the U.S. government, called his family to his deathbed.

"You now have that for which we so long and bravely fought. Keep it forever in peace and honor. Go now and rest. I shall speak to you no more."

"SHOSHONE MIKE" DAGGETT

[Near Winnemucca, Nevada, February 26, 1911]

In possibly the last Indian skirmish of the Old West, Shoshone Mike and his family, who had always avoided white society but were being accused of theft, were relentlessly pursued, Mike and his sons slain because they had recently killed four sheepherders.

"Me Shoshone! Me Shoshone! Me heap good Injun."

PIONEERS AND SETTLERS

HENRY SAGER, Pioneer
[Green River on the Oregon Trail, late August, 1844]

Just before dying from an illness called "camp fever," he turned to his little daughter, crippled weeks earlier when she fell under the wagon wheels.

"Poor child! What will become of you?"

CHARLES T. STANTON, Pioneer
[Near Truckee Lake, California, December 21, 1846]

Trapped by winter weather in the Sierra Nevada Mountains, he remained by a dying fire, unable to keep up with the exhausted and starving members of the Donner party, who asked if he were ready to continue.

"Yes, I am coming soon."

JOHN MARSHALL CLEMENS, Justice of the Peace
[Hannibal, Missouri, March 24, 1847]

Suffering from pleurisy that developed from riding twelve miles in a rain and sleet storm, the father of Mark Twain put his arm around the neck of his daughter Pamela, drew her down, and kissed her.

"Let me die."

CAPTAIN VAUGHAN
[Near The Dalles, Oregon Territory, October 1849]

As he and his six-man crew approached Cascade Falls on the Columbia River, the men tried to convince him to land the raft.

"No, I'm going to run her on down, if I run her to purgatory."

MARY ANN OATMAN, Captive
[Mojave Village, on the Colorado River, autumn 1853]

Three years after she and her sister, Olive, were captured by Apaches who murdered their parents and then traded the girls to the Mojave tribe, Mary Ann, about ten years old, died of malnutrition, quietly singing songs as she lay weakening.

"Olive, I shall die soon. You will live and get away."

MRS. HARVEY JONES, Pioneer
[Puget Sound settlement, near Seattle, Oregon Territory, summer 1855]

Attacked by Muckleshoot Indians, dying Mrs. Jones was found by her three children, led by seven-year-old son Johnny, who had returned to their burned home after they had escaped the attack.

"Johnny, Johnny, take care of them—
the Indians will kill us all if you stay here."

JOHN MARSH, Doctor/Rancher
[Near Martinez, California, September 1856]

On his way to meet his new bride, he was stopped by three vaqueros who were impatient for their wages and who, probably thinking the equally impatient Marsh was carrying a good deal of money for his journey to San Francisco, slit Marsh's throat.

"I'll pay you tomorrow when I return from San Francisco."

SMITH HOLLOWAY, Pioneer
[Battle Mountain, Nevada, August 14, 1857]

Asserting his independence, he and two other families camped away from the wagon train despite the warning that they would be vulnerable to Indians who, indeed, did attack as soon as Holloway greeted the morning.

"Wake up, everyone. No redskins in sight!"

JACOB GANTZ, German Immigrant
[Denver, Colorado, July 20, 1860]

Asked to have a drink with drunken James Gordon, Gantz refused, angering Gordon, who knocked Gantz down, pointed his revolver at Gantz's head, and pulled the trigger five times before a shell exploded, killing Gantz.

"For God's sake, don't kill me!"

LOREN WISEMAN, Pioneer Child
[Near St. James, Nebraska, July 26, 1863]

Along with five siblings, ages eight to sixteen, four-year-old Loren was attacked by Indians while the parents were away. All the children died, Loren dying from his stab wounds three days after the attack.

"The Indians scared me."

WILLIAM PHILLIPS
[Near Elk City, Idaho Territory, October 11, 1863]

He shouted his last word as his murderers, having already killed Lloyd Magruder and three other travelling companions, readied the ax for a second blow.

"Murder!"

TOM "DOC" WILSON, Settler
[Near Fort Belknap, Texas, October 13, 1864]

Fleeing Comanche Indians, he, with Thomas and Thornton Hamby, alighted in a neighbor's yard, only to receive an arrow in his heart as he got to the door.

"Hamby, I am a dead man."

GIOVANNI MARIE AUGUSTINO
"The Hermit"
[Near Mesilla, New Mexico, April 17, 1869]

After years of wandering throughout South and North America, the Italian holy man and missionary, who preferred living in solitude on mountains, was found dead, pierced by arrows. The day before his death, he informed Father Baca that he was departing for Old Mexico the next day. The signal fire was a device he often used in other places with other people.

"Tonight I will be in my cave and will build my last fire to bid you goodbye. I will pray my rosary and I want you to do likewise with your people on the roofs of your houses. If you don't see the fire you may know that I am dead and may come tomorrow and get my books and property."

S. H. WALL, Sheepman
[Arapahoe County, Colorado, September 17, 1871]

Shot several times by two thieves, he fled on foot down a dry riverbed, but, weak and exhausted, sat down and awaited the approach of his killers, who clubbed him to death.

"What have I done?"

JAMES M. HARRIS, Settler
[Near Grangeville, California, May 11, 1880]

When a U.S. Marshal and railroad land agents tried to evict settlers on railroad land, the organized settlers stopped them in a vicious gunbattle in which seven men died.

"We don't propose to injure you, but, by God, you must give up your arms!"

A. M. CONKLIN, Editor
[Socorro, New Mexico, December 24, 1880]

As an elder of the church, Conklin, editor of the *Socorro Sun*, was instrumental in ousting from the evening church service the Baca brothers, who had caused a commotion and who then waited for Conklin and shot him as he was leaving the services.

"May the Lord have mercy on my soul."

DOLL SMITH, Rancher
[Hamilton, Texas, May 1, 1881]

Smith's simple request that two cowboys move their horses so that he could load his wagon resulted in an argument and a fight in which Smith was shot and killed.

"What are you doing that for? I haven't anything against you, or you against me. I don't know you!"

BEN FROST, Rancher
[Near Little Lake, California, March 12, 1882]

Riding home with two friends, he was killed, according to the coroner's report, "by a shot from a pistol in the cantinas on the saddle of John Robertson's horse, accidentally discharged by the horse shaking itself."

"Who fired that pistol?"

HORACE W. MATHEWS, Miner
[Near Leadville, Colorado, February 21, 1885]

Before an avalanche engulfed the cabin in which he and nine other miners died, he wrote a letter.

"Snow, snow, snow! Will it ever stop?"

"AUNT" CLARA BROWN
[Denver, Colorado, October 23, 1885]

Born a slave, this Colorado pioneer, who eventually became a laundress, entrepreneur, unofficial social worker, and nurse, died peacefully in bed at the age of eighty-three.

"Mammy, Mammy!"

EDWARD H. TOWNSEND, Storekeeper
[Todd, Oklahoma Territory, March 28, 1894]

Just before two more robbers gained entrance to his home, he trustingly fed their accomplice and played the good host.

"Where is your home?"

WILFORD HAFEN, Pioneer Child
[Bunkerville, Nevada, spring 1896]

Having caught measles on a family visit, eight-year-old Wilford suffered "smothering spells" and died after continually looking up at the corner of the ceiling, where he appeared to address his final words.

"I'm coming."

EMMA FRENCH
[Winslow, Arizona, November 16, 1897]

Pioneer, self-taught doctor, widow number sixteen of Mormon John Doyle Lee, "Grandma" French, sensing her own death, turned to her second husband of twenty years before collapsing.

"Oh, Frank."

ZEB CLEUER
[Insane asylum, Utah, fall, 1903]

Always "possessed by devils," he died believing he was seeing his faithful dog, Blackie, who had been his inseparable companion before confinement in the asylum. Blackie was found dead at the farm the day after Zeb died.

"Here, big boy! Here, Blackie. Come with Zeb."

FRIENDLY DUBOSE, Pioneer
[Alice, Texas, 1909]

Minutes before he died, the old Civil War veteran, rancher, stage driver, and justice of the peace asked for a can in which to urinate.

"Thank you, Charlie. Now I am easy and can die like a man."

THE MONTANA HANGINGS

GEORGE IVES, Murderer
[Nevada City, Montana, December 21, 1863]

Found guilty of murder, he was quickly hanged, this execution giving the Montana citizens the courage to begin a two-month lynching spree.

"I am innocent of this crime. Alex Carter killed the Dutchman. Tell my mother I died an innocent man."

In January and February, 1864, the "good people" of the mining towns of Bannack and Virginia City, Montana, took the law into their own hands. Using a list purportedly given to them by one of their first victims, Red Yeager, the vigilantes deliberately set out to rid their area of a gang of criminals whose leader was supposedly the sheriff of Bannack, Henry Plummer. The lack of evidence never concerned the vigilantes. In all, twenty-one men were lynched.

GEORGE BROWN, Rancher
[Laurin's Ranch, Stinkingwater Valley, Montana, January 4, 1864]

Although accused of being a "gang member," he was probably innocent, his association with Red Yeager being evidence enough for the vigilantes to hang him.

"God Almighty, save my soul."

ERASTUS "RED" YEAGER
[Laurin's Ranch, Stinkingwater Valley, Montana, January 4, 1864]

Before being hanged by the vigilantes, he desperately gave them what they wanted, a list of "gang members," though it is doubtful that the men on the list were part of an organized gang.

"Goodbye, boys. God bless you. You are on a good undertaking."

HENRY PLUMMER, Sheriff
[Bannack, Montana, January 10, 1864]

On a makeshift gallows, preferring a broken neck to slow strangulation, he made his last request to the vigilantes, who suspected him of illegal activities.

"Give me a high drop, men."

ED RAY, Deputy
[Bannack, Montana, January 10, 1864]

Hanged along with Sheriff Plummer, and for the same reasons, he was quickly hoisted up before he could finish praying.

"Hold on, damn it! You're choking me!"

"DUTCH" JOHN WAGNER
[Bannack, Montana, January 11, 1864]

One of the names on Yeager's list, he was hanged by the vigilantes, who suspected him of robbery and other crimes.

"I have never seen a man hanged. How long will it take me to die?"

GEORGE LANE, Shoemaker
[Virginia City, Montana, January 14, 1864]

Noose in place, he leaped off his box, unable to bear waiting for the vigilantes to kick out the boxes from under four other condemned men.

"Believe in my innocence! I'm not able to witness their deaths!"

JACK GALLAGHER, Outlaw
[Virginia City, Montana, January 14, 1864]

With a vigilante noose around his neck, he took a shot of whiskey.

"How do I look, boys, with a halter around my neck?"

BOONE HELM, Outlaw
[Virginia City, Montana, January 14, 1864]

Probably the worst of the group, he was strung up beside Jack Gallagher and given a last request.

"Well, then, I want one more drink of whiskey before I die."

[After drinking] *"Let her rip! Hurrah for Jeff Davis! Every man for his principles!"*

ASA HAYES LYONS
[Virginia City, Montana, January 14, 1864]

He was the last of the five to be hanged together by the vigilantes in Virginia City.

"Give Caroline back her gold watch and tell her to take care of my body, and not to leave me hanging long."

STEPHEN MARSHLAND
[Near Virginia City, Montana, January 16, 1864]

Suspected, probably unjustly, of robbery, he was caught by the vigilantes in their cleanup of the area and strung up.

"Have mercy on me for my youth!"

WILLIAM BUNTON, Saloon/Store Owner
[Cottonwood, Montana, January 19, 1864]

Deemed a bad character, he was put on a box with a vigilante noose around his neck.

"It may never be known in this world, but in the next it will be proved that I have never committed a crime or been guilty of an act unjustified. But since I am to be hanged, I am sorry that I cannot leap from a precipice five hundred feet high instead of being forced to make such a short, uncertain jump."

GEORGE SHEARS, Horse Thief
[Bitterroot Valley, Montana, January 24, 1864]

At the request of the vigilantes, he climbed a ladder and put his head in the noose, which had been thrown over a barn beam.

"Gentlemen, I'm not used to this business, never having been hanged before. Shall I jump off or slide off? ... All right. Goodbye."

ALEXANDER CARTER
[Hell Gate, Montana, January 25, 1864]

Accused of a murder that he claimed was self-defense, he kept calm, wryly commenting until the vigilantes told him to shut up.

"Well, then, let's have a smoke ... I am innocent."

CYRUS SKINNER, Saloonkeeper
[Hell Gate, Montana, January 25, 1864]

Since his livelihood put him in constant contact with outlaws, he was scooped up when the vigilantes cleaned up Hell Gate.

"I am innocent!"

ROBERT ZACHARY
[Hell Gate, Montana, January 25, 1864]

Accused of robbery, he wrote a long letter to his family, then prayed before his lynching.

"Forgive the Vigilance Committee."

JOHNNIE COOPER
[Hell Gate, Montana, January 25, 1864]

Wounded and unable to walk, the accused robber was taken on a sled to the same soapboxes where his uncle Cyrus Skinner had recently been hanged.

"I want a good smoke before I die. I always did enjoy a smoke."

GAMBLERS

ANONYMOUS RIVERBOAT CAPTAIN
[Mississippi River, c. 1840s]

After losing, with four kings, his two-thirds interest in his steamboat in a crooked poker game, he went to his stateroom, wrote a letter, and shot himself.

"A man who would bet his last dollar on four kings doesn't deserve standing room on earth."

OLIVER RUCKER, Gambler
[Salt Lake City, Utah, 1858]

Shot and stabbed during a gambling argument with gambler Langford Peel, he wanted his money sent to his mother.

"Tell her I'm dead, but for God's sake don't break her heart telling her I went like this."

DAVIS K. TUTT, Gambler
[Springfield, Missouri, July 21, 1865]

Though a gambling friend of Wild Bill Hickok, Tutt quarreled with Hickok over a gambling debt. Meeting on the public square, they drew and fired, Tutt clutching his chest, running a few steps, and then falling, killed by Hickok with one shot at a distance of seventy-five yards.

"Boys, I am killed!"

FERD PATTERSON, Gambler
[Walla Walla, Washington, February 15, 1866]

His enemy, Tom Donahue, confronted him, saying that one of them must kill the other.

"Certainly, Donahue, I'll be glad to oblige you, but at present I am unarmed. My guns are over at the Idle Hour."

BOB POTEE, Gambler
[Kansas City, Missouri, 1883]

Before dressing in his finest clothes and walking casually into the Missouri River, he left a note for his friend Joe Bassett.

"Plant me decently, Joe."

JOHN HENRY "DOC" HOLLIDAY, Gambler
[Glenwood Springs, Colorado, November 8, 1887]

The fearless dentist-turned-gambler, participant in many deadly encounters including the gunfight at the OK Corral, died of tuberculosis in his hotel bed.

"This is funny."

JAMES DUNLEAVY, Gambler
[Tucson, Arizona, January 1888 (?)]

Challenged to a gun duel because of a gambling argument, he was caught unaware by his opponent, accompanied by several friends who fired twelve bullets into him.

"I am unarmed, you cowardly sons of bitches!"

CLIFF SPARKS, Gambler
[Denver, Colorado, 1892]

After being shot by Tom Cady, he was told by a friend in colorful horse race metaphor that he was dying.

"I'm last."

JIM BURKE, Gambler
[Merced, California, June, 1894]

Stabbed by an irate patron, he refused to identify his assailant to the authorities.

"If I live, I want to kill him, and if I die I don't want him prosecuted."

HARRY T. HAYWARD, Gambler
[Minneapolis, Minnesota, December 11, 1895]

After buying two insurance policies on Kitty Ging and then arranging her murder, the gambler went poker-faced to the gallows.

"Pull her tight. I'll stand pat."

JOHN E. PRYDE, Lumbercamp Cook
[Brainerd, Minnesota, July 23, 1896]

Having lost his money gambling, he killed a logger for $41 and went to the scaffold.

[Eve of execution] *"Nothing but gambling has brought me to this. I hope every gambling hell in this city may be closed by law and kept closed."*

[On the scaffold] *"God forgive me for my sins, and save my soul for my Savior's sake. Amen."*

POLICY BOB, Down-and-Out Gambler
[Nome, Alaska, c. 1900]

Lying in an opium delirium, he still hoped to win with a big bet at Faro.

"Copper the deuce! Copper the deuce!"

SOLDIERS AND SCOUTS

EDWARD F. STOREY, Captain
[Pinnacle Mount, Nevada, June 8, 1860]

Mortally wounded in a skirmish with Piute Indians near Pyramid
Lake, Storey received all the consideration his men could con-
ceive, including the gift of the scalp of the Indian who had shot
him.

*"Take it away. Why should I want to see it? Tell me about the
Rifles. How are my men faring?"*

JAMES "PADDY" GRAYDON, Captain, U.S. Cavalry
[Fort Stanton, New Mexico, November 5, 1862]

After suffering a day of accusations, he shot it out with Dr.
Whitlock.

"The damned rascal has killed me!"

STEPHEN WATSON, Second Lieutenant
[Near the future Camp Maury, Oregon, May 18, 1864]

Moments before being shot in the face, Watson led his thirteen men in an attack against the Snake Indians.

"Pour it into them, boys!"

SIGMUND STERNBERG, Lieutenant
[Near Fort C. F. Smith, Montana, August 1, 1867]

In charge of a detail of soldiers protecting haycutters during an attack by Sioux warriors, he tried to set an example for his men, who took shelter behind logs. Apparently, though, the men were not impressed when Sternberg took a bullet in the head.

"Stand up, men, and fight like soldiers!"

MICHAEL MEARA, Sergeant
[Infernal Caverns, Modoc County, California, September 27, 1867]

On foot, climbing in pursuit of Indians who were hiding in rocky terrain, he spied the enemy through a fissure and was immediately shot in the head.

"Here they are, boys!"

CHRISTOPHER "KIT" CARSON, Frontiersman
[Fort Lyons, Colorado, May 28, 1868]

After a lifetime on the frontier as mountain man, army scout, and Indian fighter, he died in the surgeon's quarters of an aneurysm at the age of fifty-eight.

[Last Letter]
Mouth of Purgatoire River
May 5th, 1868
Dear Compadre: [His nephew, Aloys Scheurich]
I have received your letter and it has been a satisfaction to me to hear that you are all well. I arrived here on the 11th of last month, sick and worn out, but began to improve from that time and would be comparatively healthy if the misfortune, losing my wife hadn't happened. Those were trying days for me. My health is improving now and I am very apt to be on the other side of the mountains by the end of this month; it is almost necessary for me to go, as much on account of business as for the sake of my health, to avoid the heat during the summer months.

You have had before this the particulars of my wife's death and I need not repeat them here. My children are all well.

We are farming as much as can be done without going to any great expense. I had a ditch taken out and everything works well in that respect. I intended to build me a house, but as I apprehend some trouble about our land, I decided to wait until matters are settled.

Now I have told you of my intentions and prospects, I expect you will appreciate the interest I am taking in you and yours and let me know what your calculations are for the future.

It is my intention to send my wife's corpse to Taos, as soon as the weather is cool enough to do so and have taken the necessary steps to have this done, even if I myself should be called away, she shall rest as close to her family as possible. I have given the necessary orders to have my own body, if I should die, and that of my wife's sent together to Taos, to be buried in our graveyard near Elfego. I want neither her nor myself to be buried in the Church.

My best regards to the old lady, [Mrs. Bent] Terresina and your boy, who I am told is a fine child.

Please tell the old lady that there is nobody in the world who can take care of my children but her and she must know that it would be the greatest of favors to me, if she would come and stay until I am healthier and may make such arrangements as would suit her. She has two children here and is among those nearest to her.

The country has not changed much since she was here last, no danger of Indians now. A greater number of people are living here, than then.

If she should determine to come, let me know immediately, and I will send a carriage for her. Chipita Gorda is nursing the baby, which is doing very well, but still I am anxious to get another nurse.

Remember me to all my friends, more particularly Miller, and don't delay to give an answer.

> *Yours truly*
> *C. Carson*

[Dying] *"Doctor, compadre, adios."*

KIRK GORDON, Guide
[Near Fort Dodge, Kansas, September 1868]

When members of a wagon train refused to rescue a woman who was being tortured by Indians within screaming distance, he rode in alone, scooping her up and returning her safely by protecting her with his body, which received several mortal wounds.

"Stick to the horse whatever happens!"

FREDERICK BEECHER, Lieutenant
[Beecher's Island, Colorado, September 17, 1868]

After the first fierce attack by Roman Nose's Cheyenne warriors, he reported to his commander and collapsed.

"I have my death wound, general. Good night."

LOUIS MALONE HAMILTON, Captain
[Battle of the Washita, Oklahoma, November 27, 1868]

Assigned to protect the supply wagons, he convinced Custer to let him participate in the battle and was killed as the charge began toward Black Kettle's village.

"Now, men, keep cool, fire low, and not too rapidly."

JOEL ELLIOT, Major, U.S. Cavalry
[Battle of the Washita, Oklahoma, November 27, 1868]

Before he and his small detachment were killed chasing Indians who were escaping from Black Kettle's village, he shouted to another officer:

"Here's for a brevet or a coffin!"

PETER WELSH, Private
[Hays, Kansas, September 6, 1873]

Welsh and Private George H. Sumner, soldiers from Fort Hays, were both killed while arguing with another private during a night on the town.

"Oh, don't hurt me!"

JAMES MALONE, Private
[Prescott, Arizona, March 21, 1878]

Found guilty of murder in a civil court, he was hanged.

"Since I can do no good in this world, maybe I can in another."

JONATHAN "BUFFALO CHIPS" WHITE, Scout
[Slim Buttes, South Dakota, September 9, 1876]

When General Crook attacked Sioux warriors, his scout, an imitator of Buffalo Bill, ignored warnings in his eagerness to kill Indians and was shot in the heart.

"Oh Lord! They've got me now, boys!"

CHARLES BLEWETT, Army Scout
[Near Cottonwood, Idaho, July 4, 1877]

Ambushed by Nez Perce, shortly before he was killed he responded to his partner's warning that they must escape.

"Not until I get me an Indian."

EDMUND C. HENTIG, Captain
[Near Fort Apache, Arizona, August 30, 1881]

As the military column camped for the night with an important Apache captive, Hentig, on his final western detail, attempted to prevent Apache warriors from entering the camp, his death setting off a battle.

"Ucashay!" [Go away!]

MELVILLE CARY WILKINSON, Major
[Sugar Point, Leech Lake, Minnesota, October 5, 1898]

In the last pitched battle between Indians and the U.S. Army, set off when the army tried to find a fugitive whom the band was hiding, the major received two minor wounds before receiving a mortal wound.

"I'm hit, Ross, but not badly. Keep 'em at it!"

BAPTISTE "LITTLE BAT" GARNIER, Guide/Scout
[Crawford, Nebraska, December 16, 1900]

Part French, part Sioux, this skillful tracker got caught up in the prejudices of a new community where white men, Indians, cowboys, black soldiers, and mixed-bloods mingled. Garnier, after a show of independence, was shot by a bartender and spoke his last words in Sioux to his Sioux wife.

"I thought Haguewood was my friend,
so why would a friend shoot me?"

NO MERCY FROM THE HANGING JUDGE

In 1875 Judge Isaac C. Parker was appointed judge for the Indian Territories. From his court at Fort Smith, Arkansas, he sent out his deputy sheriffs to gather up the outlaws. He set a stern example when he sentenced to death six murderers.

JAMES MOORE, Murderer
[Fort Smith, Arkansas, September 3, 1875]

One of six murderers hanged together after the appointment of Judge Parker, "The Hanging Judge."

"I have lived like a man, and I will die like a man. . . . I see men in this crowd who are worse than I have ever been. I hope you make peace with God before brought to my condition."

SAM FOOY, Murderer
[Fort Smith, Arkansas, September 3, 1875]

He directed his last words to the crowd gathered to watch the remarkable simultaneous hanging of six murderers.

"I am as anxious to get out of this world as you are to see me go."

EDMUND CAMPBELL, Murderer
[Fort Smith, Arkansas, September 3, 1875]

On Judge Parker's gallows, he made a brief protest.

"I didn't shoot anybody. I am innocent and ready to die."

SMOKER MANKILLER, Murderer
[Fort Smith, Arkansas, September 3, 1875]

He was one of two Indians that Judge Parker made an example of on this day.

"I did not kill Short. I would admit it if I did. I stand before you convicted by prejudice and false testimony."

WILLLIAM WHITTINGTON, Murderer
[Fort Smith, Arkansas, September 3, 1875]

Although he thought that he would not have the fortitude to speak on the gallows and therefore had written a long speech that was read for him, he did manage to find his voice as the trap was sprung.

"Jesus save me!"

CRAWFORD GOLDSBY, Murderer
[Fort Smith, Arkansas, March 17, 1896]

This notorious criminal, "Cherokee Bill," recognized friends who had come to view his hanging.

"Goodbye, all you chums down that way."

THE BATTLE AT THE LITTLE BIGHORN

On June 25, 1876, Lieutenant Colonel George Armstrong Custer attacked the huge Indian village on the Little Bighorn River, Montana. He divided his command, sending Major Marcus Reno to attack on one end of the village while Custer would attack from the other end. Custer and his command of more than two hundred men were wiped out, their last words lost in the smoke of battle.

Reno attacked but was forced to retreat across the river. He and his men were fortunate to reach a hilltop, now called Entrenchment Hill, where they could defend themselves, although Indian sharpshooters killed several men. Their defense lasted two nights until the Indians departed just prior to the arrival of General Terry on the morning of June 27.

GEORGE ARMSTRONG CUSTER, Lieutenant Colonel
[Little Bighorn, Montana, June 25, 1876]

Although his last words are lost in the smoke of the charge and retreat to the hillside known as Custer's Last Stand, his last recorded words were a letter to his wife and a battlefield order to Captain Benteen, written down, and probably paraphrased, by his adjutant Cooke.

[Letter to Libbie Custer]
My Darling—I have but a few moments to write as we start at twelve, and I have my hands full of preparations for

the scout. Do not be anxious about me...I hope to have a good report sent to you by the next mail.

Your devoted boy
Autie.

[Battlefield order] *"Come on. Big village. Be quick. Bring packs."*

BENJAMIN H. "BENNY" HODGSON, Second Lieutenant
[Reno's Retreat, Little Bighorn, Montana, June 25, 1876]

Wounded, he was shot in the temple and killed just moments before his rescue could be completed by a mounted soldier dragging him from the river.

"Don't abandon me! I'm shot in both legs!"

MILES F. O'HARA, Sergeant
[Reno's Retreat, Little Bighorn, Montana, June 25, 1876]

Shot in the chest, he was unable to retreat with the others.

"For God's sake, don't leave me!"

GEORGE LORENTZ, Private
[Reno's Retreat, Little Bighorn, Montana, June 25, 1876]

After being shot in the back of the neck, he was propped against a tree by Private Morris.

"Go on, you cannot do me any good."

"Lonesome" Charley Reynolds, Scout
[Reno's Retreat, Little Bighorn, Montana, June 25, 1876]

As the soldiers began to retreat, he saw Doctor Porter aiding a fallen soldier.

"Let's go, Doctor! Everybody's leaving! ... Be careful.
The Indians are shooting at you!"

Isaiah "Teat" Dorman, Interpreter
[Reno's Retreat, Little Bighorn, Montana, June 25, 1876]

As Dorman, the only black man in the battle, retreated, his wounded horse fell. Dorman knelt, firing at the Indians as Private Rutten rode by. Surrounded, Dorman was mortally wounded and made a request of the Sioux, with whom he was once friendly. The request was ignored; Dorman's body was mutilated.

"Goodbye, Rutten!"

[Later] *"My friends, you have already killed me;*
don't count coup on me."

·Henry M. Cody, Corporal
[Reno's Retreat, Little Bighorn, Montana, June 25, 1876]

Too wounded to escape from the Indians, even when assisted, he watched other soldiers retreat.

"Goodbye, boys!"

68

LAME WHITE MAN, Cheyenne Leader
[Little Bighorn, Montana, June 25, 1876]

Seeing a troop of soldiers riding into an exposed position, he rallied the warriors near him.

"Come! We can kill all of them!"

DEWITT WINNEY, First Sergeant K Company
[Sharpshooter's Ridge, Little Bighorn, Montana, June 25, 1876]

Raising his head for a look, he stared bewilderedly, shot in the forehead.

"I am hit!"

JAMES J. TANNER, Private
[Entrenchment Hill, Little Bighorn, Montana, June 26, 1876]

Having been rescued from the field by his friend Private Newell, he was taken to the field hospital where, just before he died, he responded to Newell's comment that "They got you."

"No, but they will in a few minutes."

GEORGE LELL, Corporal
[Entrenchment Hill, Little Bighorn, Montana, June 26, 1876]

Mortally wounded and taken to the field hospital, he made a last request.

"Lift me up, boys; I want to see the boys again before I go."

BANDITS AND THIEVES

FELIPE ESPINOSA, Outlaw
[Near Fort Garland, Colorado, September, 10, 1863]

Surprised at his cabin, he just had time to utter a warning to his nephew before Tom Tobin shot him, then decapitated him, taking the head for identification.

"Jesus favor me! Escape, I am killed!"

TIBURCIO VASQUEZ, Outlaw
[San Jose, California, March 19, 1875]

The night before his execution, the notorious outlaw asked to see his satin-lined coffin, which was then brought to his cell. Later he was asked if he believed in an afterlife.

[Viewing coffin] *"I can sleep here forever very well!"*

[Later, re. afterlife] *"I hope so, for in that case by tomorrow I will see all my old sweethearts together!"*

[On the gallows] *"Pronto!"*

ANONYMOUS MEXICAN BANDIT
[Texas-Mexico border, near Brownsville, Texas, June 12, 1875]

Having his horse shot from under him as he tried to escape from Texas Rangers, he crawled into a thicket where, with a knife, he confronted his pursuer, Ranger Captain McNelly, who put his last bullet into the bandit.

"Me gotta you now; me gotta you."

CHARLIE PITTS, Outlaw
[Near Medalia, Minnesota, September 21, 1876]

As a posse closed in on him and the Younger brothers after the Northfield Raid, Pitts responded to Cole Younger's thoughts of death.

"All right, Captain, I can die as game as you can.
Let's get it done."

SAM BASS, Outlaw
[Round Rock, Texas, July 21, 1878]

After being shot by a posse, he lingered in pain but made a statement concerning men involved in a robbery.

"These men were Joel Collins, Bill Heffridge, Tom Nixon, Jack Davis, Jim Berry and me. Tom Nixon is in Canada. Haven't seen him since that robbery. Jack Davis was in New Orleans from the time of that robbery till he went to Denton to get me to go with him to buy hides. This was the last of April, 1878. About the shooting at Round Rock. Grimes asked me if I had a pistol. Said I did, then all three of us drew and shot him. If I killed him it was the first man I ever killed.

I am twenty-seven years old. Have four sisters and brothers. John and Linton at Mitchell, Indiana. Have not seen Underwood since the Salt Creek fight. Saw two Collinses at old man Collins' since I left Denton. Have been in the robbing business a long time. Had done much business of that kind before the U. P. robbery last fall."

[Later, told that he was dying] *"Let me go!...The world is bobbing around me."*

BILL BRAZELTON, Stagecoach Robber
[Near Tucson, Arizona, August 19, 1878]

Having concealed his identity by wearing a white flour sack during robberies, he baffled lawmen until an expert tracker spotted his horse's prints in Tucson. An accomplice who was supposed to bring supplies to Brazelton was convinced to take a posse to the evening rendezvous where Brazelton, surprised, was shot down.

"You son of a bitch! I'll die brave! My God, I'll pray till I die."

WILLIAM C. JONES, Stagecoach Robber
[Near Wellington Station, Nevada, September 5, 1880]

About four o'clock in the morning, Jones and companions tried to hold up the Bodie-Carson City stage. Jones was drawn into the open by Wells Fargo messenger Mike Tovey, who, shotgun in hand, pretended that he was frightened and unarmed.

"Don't move or I'll murder every last—"

JESSE JAMES, Outlaw
[St. Joseph, Missouri, April 3, 1882]

Perhaps attempting to convince young Bob Ford of the insignificance of Jesse's suspicions aroused by a newspaper article and possibly thinking that Ford would not try anything in the

Jameses' house with family present, Jesse took off his guns and turned his back on Ford in order to adjust or dust a picture.

Jesse James is included here only to dispel a myth. There are no recorded last words by him. At the coroner's inquest, even his killer, Bob Ford, does not state James' last words. The most commonly published version of James' last words ("That picture looks awful dusty.") is a fabrication by author Carl W. Breihan, who wrote many articles dramatizing the life of the outlaw.

BRACK CORNETT, Train Robber
[Allee's Ranch, near Pearsall, Texas, February 12, 1888]

Probably because there were many rewards for him, Cornett was taken unaware by rancher Alf Allee, who, at gunpoint, ordered Cornett to surrender.

"Not by a damn sight!"

ROBERT YOUNGER, Outlaw
[State Penitentiary, Stillwater, Minnesota, September 16, 1889]

One of the infamous Younger brothers, Bob, suffering from pulmonary tuberculosis, whispered to his brother, Cole, his final thoughts about Maggie, a friend from whom he had estranged himself until such time as he could be released from prison.

"Tell her I died thinking of her."

BOB DALTON, Bank Robber
[Coffeyville, Kansas, October 5, 1892]

Mortally wounded in the street during the famous raid by the Dalton gang on two Coffeyville banks, he spoke to his brother who, amid the shooting, was trying to lift him onto the horse.

"It's no use."

THE DUTCHMAN, Outlaw
[Near Norman, Oklahoma, 1892]

Having escaped from jail, the desperate Dutchman, who was probably German, broke into a store and was gutshot by a night watchman. Captured several hours later, he lay dying in a barn and was asked if he wanted a priest.

"A priest! What could a priest do? Send me to purgatory? I don't want to go to purgatory—I want to go to hell!"

ART FRIAR, Horse Thief
[Nogallitos Pass, Texas, September 28, 1896]

Wounded twice, he used his last words as a ruse to draw from their cover two Texas Rangers, who promptly killed him when he fired at them.

"I have got enough."

GEORGE BAIN, Bank Robber
[Meeker, Colorado, October 13, 1896]

He was shot during an unsuccessful bank robbery.

"Oh, mother!"

WILL CARVER, Outlaw
[Sonora, Texas, April 2, 1901]

The noted outlaw, former companion of Butch Cassidy and the Wild Bunch, raved deliriously after being mortally wounded resisting arrest.

"Keep shelling them, boys! Will you stay with me? Will you swear it? Stay with the safe! Now we have them! Die game!"

TOM JORDAN, Bank Robber
[Keystone, Oklahoma, May 8, 1911]

He was shot down in the bank by Sheriff Marshall, who, prepared for the robbery, told Jordan to hold up his hands.

"Hold up your own hands!"

RODRIGUEZ RAMIREZ, Bandit Leader
[Glen Springs, Texas, May 6, 1916]

Leading a group of inebriated Mexican bandits, he was shot down while attacking a small detachment of soldiers.

"Mueran los gringos!" [Kill the Americans!]

LEGAL HANGINGS

JOSEFA, Dance Hall Girl
[Downieville, California, July 5, 1851]

Having knifed to death a miner the day before, the Mexican woman was given a speedy miners' trial and hanged despite the fact that women were a rarity in the gold fields. She bravely put the noose around her neck and threw her hat to a friend.

"Adiós, señores."

ANN BILANSKY, Murderer
[St. Paul, Minnesota, March 23, 1860]

Guilty of poisoning her husband with arsenic, she went to the gallows alone. Her lover was not arrested.

"I die without having had any mercy shown me, or justice. I die for the good of my soul, and not for murder. May you all profit by my death. Your courts of justice are not courts of justice—but I will yet get justice in heaven. I am a guilty woman, I know, but not of this murder, which was committed by another. I forgive every body who did me wrong. I die a sacrifice to the law. I hope you all may be judged better than I have been, and by a more righteous judge. I die

prepared to meet my God. [To the deputy] *How can you
stain your hands by putting that rope around my neck—the
instrument of my death? Be sure my face is well covered.
Lord Jesus Christ, receive my soul."*

JAMES GORDON
[Denver, Colorado, October 6, 1860]

Convicted by a People's Court of murdering Jacob Gantz, he was
hanged at sunset.

*"Oh, if some good friend would only shoot me. . . . But, it is
well . . . Goodbye. Mr. Middaugh, please remember to fix the
knot so it will break my neck instantly. Oh, God, have
mercy!"*

DAVID RENTON, Outlaw
[Lewiston, Idaho Territory, March 4, 1864]

Convicted for his part in the murder of Lloyd Magruder and four
other men, he was a participant in the first legal hanging in Idaho
Territory.

*"As I expect to meet my God, I am innocent of this murder.
My hands were never imbued in human blood."*

JAMES ROMAIN, Outlaw
[Lewiston, Idaho Territory, March 4, 1864]

On the same scaffold as Renton, he accused Billy Page, the main
witness to the Magruder murders.

*"This is not a court. It is nothing but a mob. Page is guilty
of murder . . . You know that I am innocent! What I have
told you is true!"*

GEORGE CHRISTOPHER LOWREY, Outlaw
[Lewiston, Idaho Territory, March 4, 1864]

On the scaffold with his fellow murderers, Renton and Romain, he impressed the sheriff with his fortitude.

"All ready! Launch your boat!
She is nothing but an old mud-scow anyway!"

JAKE SILVIE, Murderer
[Helena, Montana, fall 1864]

Found guilty of murder, he was quickly taken to the gallows.

"Boys, don't let me hang more than two or three days."

ANDREAS ROESCH
[St. Peter, Minnesota, March 6, 1868]

The Swiss immigrant was hanged for murdering a sixteen-year-old hunter, beating the boy to death with the boy's rifle.

"Ach, Gott in Himmel!" [God in heaven!]

JOHN CHILDERS, Murderer
[Fort Smith, Arkansas, August 15, 1873]

On the gallows, discarding his cigar, he responded to the marshal's promise not to hang him if he revealed the names of other gang members.

"Didn't you say you were going to hang me?
Then, why in hell don't you?"

JOHN BOYER
[Cheyenne, Wyoming, April 21, 1871]

Having killed the two men who had raped his sister and mother, Boyer, the son of a French-Canadian trapper, became the first person legally hanged in Wyoming Territory.

> *"Look at me! I no cry. I no woman.*
> *I man! I die brave!"*

WILLIAM WILSON, Cowboy
[Lincoln, New Mexico, December 10, 1875]

On the scaffold for killing Robert Casey, Wilson directed his final words to Major L. G. Murphy, who may have been the instigator of the Casey murder. Murphy triggered the trapdoor before Wilson finished speaking.

> *"Major, you know you are the cause of this.*
> *You promised to save me, but. ..."*

Cut down too soon, he had to be taken from his coffin and hanged again.

JOHN "JACK" McCALL
[Yankton, Dakota Territory, March 1, 1877]

On the scaffold for the murder of Wild Bill Hickok:

> *"Draw it tighter, marshal ... Oh God!"*

BROWN BOWEN, Gunman
[Gonzales, Texas, May 17, 1878]

Found guilty of murdering a sleeping man, he insisted that his brother-in-law, the notorious John Wesley Hardin, had done the killing. On the gallows, he confronted the brother of the murdered man.

"Do you believe that I killed your brother?"

[Brother: "I do."] *"You believe a doggone lie."*

CICERO C. SIMMS
[Fairplay, Colorado, July 23, 1880]

Convicted of murdering John Johnson, he was legally hanged.

"I don't know as I have much to say. I have my life taken, and I do not think I have had a fair trial or a fair show, but I am willing to forgive all who had a hand in it, if they will forgive me. I hope the Lord will forgive me my sins."

ALEXANDER HARE, Outlaw
[New Westminster, British Columbia, January 31, 1881]

On the scaffold after a murderous spree with the McLean brothers, seventeen-year-old Hare was remorseful.

"I forgive everyone and thank everyone for their kindness. I am guilty of the crimes laid to my charge and justly deserve the impending punishment."

JOSEPH CASEY, Outlaw
[Tucson, Arizona, April 15, 1884]

On the scaffold for killing a jailer during a jailbreak, the cowboy waited calmly till the hood was in place.

"Turn her loose! Goodbye!"

DENNIS W. DILDA, Murderer
[Prescott, Arizona, February 5, 1886]

On the scaffold, Dilda, a predator, took advantage of the sheriff's offer of anything Dilda might want, guzzling half a pint.

"Send my body to my wife . . . " [Sheriff's offer] *"A drink."*

JOHN OWENS, Murderer
[Buffalo, Wyoming, March 5, 1886]

Having murdered a man over a five-dollar transaction, he went to the gallows with a show of bravado.

"What time is it? I wish you'd hurry up.
I want to get to hell in time for dinner."

DAMIAN ROMERO
[Springer, New Mexico, February 2, 1883]

Found guilty of murder, the eighteen-year-old Romero was hanged in public, his death witnessed by 550 people enjoying the picnic atmosphere of the event.

> *"Well, gentlemen, all I have to say is that I am not afraid to die because I am not guilty ..."*

[Shaking hands with Sheriff Mace Bowman]
> *"I will meet you in heaven."*

[Just before the drop] *"Goodbye all! I am going to Mora* [New Mexico, his birthplace] *tonight."*

MILTON J. YARBERRY, Constable
[Albuquerque, New Mexico, February 9, 1883]

Having previously been acquitted for shooting young Harry Brown, perhaps in cold blood, Yarberry was on the gallows, guilty of murder in the careless and hasty shooting of Charles Campbell.

> *"Well, Milt, they are going to hang you. Yes, they are going to hang you because you killed a son of Governor Brown of Tennessee.*
>
> *There is a man in the crowd yonder; his name is Colonel Bell. Now, Colonel, don't attempt to hide away so I can't see you. Well, this man Bell, he is a brother of Judge Bell ... Well, this man Bell went down to Silver City and while he was there he had a talk with Sheriff Whitehill of Grant County about my killing Campbell and he said: "Yes, and the damn son of a bitch will be hung and he deserves hanging and will be hung because he killed a son of Governor Brown of Tennessee." Sheriff Whitehill, he told Colonel Bell that I did right in killing Campbell and ought not to be hung for it. He said Campbell was a desperate man and I*

should have been rewarded for killing him, instead of being hung for it. Campbell was a murderer ...

Whitehill telegraphed all this to Knaebel, but it did no good because they were bound to hang me, not because I didn't do just what any other man would have done, not because I didn't act in defense of my own life, but because I killed that man Brown and he was a son of Governor Brown of Tennessee ...

I didn't want no row with Brown, but I wasn't going to hide from him or keep in any backrooms out of his sight. When I did kill him I did it in defense of my life and I was tried and acquitted. But they are determined to hang Milt and they are going to do it ...

He shot at me and I shot back ... Let me finish this...How near is the time, Perfecto? ... Gentlemen, you are hanging an innocent man."

LEE SHELLENBERGER, Farmer
[Nebraska City, Nebraska, July 23, 1887]

While waiting for a new trial on the charge of murdering his eleven-year-old daughter, he was taken from the jail by a lynch mob whom he threatened with his last breath.

> *"If there is such a thing as haunts, I will do it,*
> *for I recognize several of you."*

ANONYMOUS MURDERER
[Yuma Penitentiary Graveyard, Yuma, Arizona, c. 1887]

Just before being hanged, he was asked why he was smiling.

> *"Well, I was just thinking. You guys have got to walk*
> *back up there in this heat. I don't."*

JOHN LEE, Murderer
[Alexandria, Minnesota, February 15, 1889]

Having murdered a rival suitor a year earlier, Lee and his accomplice walked to the gallows. On the way, his accomplice received news of a commuted sentence, and Lee died alone.

*"I know my sins are forgiven and in ten minutes
I shall be in a better place."*

DAVE WALKER, Vigilante
[Ozark, Missouri, May 10, 1889]

Convicted of one of the Bald Knobber murders, he went to the gallows with his son and another Bald Knobber.

"I have no further statement, other than what I made on the stand at the trial. I was there when the men were killed, but as God is my judge and as I hope to meet Him, I did not take part in the killing but tried to prevent it.

The men who were most directly implicated in the murder are Peter and Lewis Davis, Bill Newton, Charles Graves, and Wiley Mathews. The first four were set free and Wiley got out, but I, who did all I could to prevent the boys from shooting, must hang.

It is hard, but I shall meet my fate as becomes a man. I was never arrested before, never appeared before a grand jury, never was sued, and never sued anybody. For forty years, I have lived in the county, and I defy any man to make any other charge than this against me."

JOHN MATHEWS, Vigilante
[Ozark, Missouri, May 10, 1889]

He was one of three Bald Knobbers convicted of murder and hanged.

"It is hard to die and leave my poor wife and nine children alone without a protector. There's my little baby, born two months after I was placed in the cell. It will never know it had a father. My family is in pitiable condition. James, my oldest boy, has been all spring circulating a petition to the governor to commute our sentences and could not attend to the farm. The smaller boys have tried to plant something, but I am told the farm is in a sorry way. I do not know what they will do. It makes it so much harder to die, knowing that they may suffer for food. Oh, it is hard, so hard!

Holding up my right hand, and as I expect in a few minutes to meet my Maker, I swear to you I am an innocent man. My poor wife and children and my poor old mother...."

[Hood placed] *"Oh, God, did I ever think I would die like this?"*

BILLY WALKER, Vigilante
[Ozark, Missouri, May 10, 1889]

The third, and youngest, of the Bald Knobbers executed that day, he suffered greatly when his noose came untied and he had to be taken up and hanged again, a job which took the inexperienced sheriff twenty minutes.

"I can add little to what Father has said. He had less to do with the actual killing than I. After the bullet went through my leg, I did shoot but Green and Edens were already dead. I am satisfied to die. I know that God has forgiven my sins, and I go to Him with a clear conscience. Death has no terrors for me."

[Falls through trap to the ground] *"Oh, Lord, get it over! Get it over!"* [Responding to the crowd's call for freedom] *"Please let me go, sheriff. Then, for God's sake, hurry. God, I commit myself to Thee."*

JOHN LEHMAN, Murderer
[Custer City, South Dakota, February 19, 1892]

In the only legal hanging in Custer County, Lehman, killer of Sheriff John Burns, made comments to Reverend Tracy before being taken to the scaffold.

[To Tracy] *"Praying is not my business. That is your profession. You pray for me, and if I have done anything wrong, that will make it all right."*

[Before the drop] *"I want to say to the audience and spectators that you are cruel men and are murdering me."*

CHARLEY MILLER, Murderer
[Cheyenne, Wyoming, April 22, 1892]

Having barely survived freezing with William Kingen during a jail break, he was recaptured and hanged on a "self-hanging" scaffold run by water weights that took about sixty seconds to activate the trap.

"God have mercy on my soul ... Please be quick ... Do you want me to stand in the middle? ... This rope is choking me! ... All right ... God have mercy on me."

CHARLES BROOKS, Servant
[Spokane, Washington, September 6, 1892]

The sixty-three-year-old black man had shot his white wife on a downtown street and became the first man hanged in Spokane.

"I am going to Heaven. I'm completely ready to go, for I know I've been forgiven all my sins."

JOHN MILLIGAN, Murderer
[Oklahoma City, Oklahoma, March 13, 1895]

On the gallows, the first man legally hanged in Oklahoma Territory went to his death tight-lipped when asked if he had anything to say.

"Not a word."

WILLIAM FREDERICKS, Murderer
[San Quentin, California, July 26, 1895]

Convicted of murdering a sheriff, he walked to the scaffold knowing that a well-positioned noose meant a broken neck and instant death rather than slow strangulation.

"Make it good and tight."

WILLIAM "BILL" GAY
[Helena, Montana, June 8, 1896]

Sentenced to hang for killing a deputy, he went to the gallows after a recent illness.

[To Sheriff Ryan] *"Goodbye, but if I hadn't been sick, I would feel better, don't you know?"*

[Moments later] *"Now as I said, it seems hard that I have to die this way. I want to see the sun as long as possible. I will never see another one and I want to see this one as long as I can. Gentlemen, you are witnesses to a man being murdered. I am murdered right here."*

[To Sheriff Jurgens] *"You've got to get the rope around, haven't you? Make it solid."*

WILLIAM "STUTTERING KID" HOLT, Outlaw
[Canon City, Colorado, June 26, 1896]

On the gallows for murder, pale and frightened, his face muscles twitching, he lived up to his nickname.

"Uh . . . uh . . . uh . . . uh . . . uh . . ."

DEONICIO ROMERO, Outlaw
[Canon City, Colorado, June 26, 1896]

Asked if he had any last words on the gallows, he responded:

"No. No use."

WILLIAM M. ROE, Murderer
[Napa, California, January 15, 1897]

Convicted of murdering respected Lucina Greenwood, Roe, after a life of crime and murder, became the last man to be publicly executed in California. The four hundred invited guests were all men.

"Hello. It's kind of a monotonous show of people. Haven't much to say. I only wish to give thanks for the way I've been treated; you've treated me well. I have no creed or kin or anything like that—so I think that is all I want to say."

[To the undersheriff who was positioning the noose] *"I want you to be sure to draw that tight."*

In his will, written the eve of his death, he left his body for medical dissection in order to "aid science inasmuch as it lays within my power."

JOSEPH OTT, Farmer
[Granite Falls, Minnesota, October 20, 1898]

On the gallows for beating his wife to death, he was hanged before approximately four hundred spectators.

"I bid you all good evening."

G. E. MORRISON, Preacher
[Vernon, Texas, October 27, 1899]

Guilty for having poisoned his wife because he fell in love with another woman, he went to the gallows after writing a brief letter to one of his guards, who had requested the letter as a souvenir.

Vernon, Texas, Oct. 26, 1899

Mr. Sullivan.

Dear Sir: You have asked me to write something that you can keep to remember the occasion of our meeting. I don't know what to say to you, but I hope the following may be entirely satisfactory.

First, I believe in a future life, and I believe that men are punished for their sins of this life, and are rewarded for the good things.

Second, I believe in a general judgment, and all must stand in that day before the bar of God and be judged. I believe I have the witness of God's spirit bearing witness with my own spirit, and believe that, though God allows man's law to take my life yet he saves me, and of the future I have no fears whatever.

Now, good-bye, and may you ever be a champion of the right and an enemy of the wrong.

Your well-wisher,
G. E. Morrison

LUM YOU
[South Bend, Washington, January 31, 1902]

Despite his plea that the white man he killed was threatening him, the successful Oriental entrepreneur went to the gallows, the first and only person hanged in Pacific County, Washington.

"Goodbye, everybody, all my friends, women and men. Me wish you all good luck. Me ready to die. Me no can see. Kill me good."

AUGUSTIN CHACON, Outlaw
[Solomonville, Arizona, November 22, 1902]

Having escaped execution in 1897, he was finally caught and hanged on the scaffold, which had been built for him five years earlier.

"I consider this to be the greatest day of my life."

HILARIO HIDALGO, Murderer
[Prescott, Arizona, July 30, 1903]

On the gallows, he showed no fear as he addressed friends in the crowd and commented to his partner in crime, who was hanged beside him.

*"Adios, Frankie! ... There's our compadre Charlie ...
Adios, amigos! Adios, everybody!"*

JAMES KEFFER, Murderer
[Lander, Wyoming, September 25, 1903]

Main participant in the only legal hanging in Fremont County, Keefer seemed ready for his punishment.

"Good morning, boys! I have no ill feelings for any man in town, but do not think much of the judge, supreme court or the governor."

[Asked if he was ready.] *"Yes."*

CLAUD D. CRAWFORD, Robber
[Elk River, Minnesota, December 5, 1905]

The Philippine War veteran, involved in a robbery aboard a train, earned the noose when he killed a man.

"I wish you all good luck. These are the last words I have to say on earth. Goodbye."

HENRY "THE FLYING DUTCHMAN" WAGNER, Outlaw
[Nanaimo, British Columbia, August 28, 1913]

The innovative outlaw who used a power launch to rob coastal towns ended on the scaffold for the murder of Constable Westaway.

"Remember me to my wife. Though she had a dark skin her heart was white."

AND SOME ILLEGAL HANGINGS

JOHN BUCROFT, Gold Seeker/Robber
[Murphys Camp, California, c. 1849]

Probably one of many goldseekers who failed to strike it rich, he resorted to robbery, which, in the lawless gold camps, was dealt with harshly.

Dear Friend:

I take this opportunity of writing these few lines to you hoping to find you in good health me and Charley is sentenced to be hung today at 5 o'clock for a robbery good by give my best to Frank and Sam and Church.

John Bucroft

TOM BELL, Outlaw
[Near Stockton, California, October 4, 1856]

Captured by citizens, he was allowed to write two letters before they lynched him.

Firebaugh's Ferry, Oct. 4 '56
Mrs. Hood, my dear and only friend now in this country:

As I am not allowed the liberty of seeing you, I have been given the privilege of writing you a few lines, as I have but a few moments to live. I am at a great loss for something to say. I have been most foully betrayed. Bill and John have told things that never took place. I am accused of every robbery that has been committed for the past twelve months, which is entirely false. I have never committed but three highway robberies in my life; but still I am to blame and my fate is sealed. I am to die like a dog, and there is but one thing that grieves me, and that is the condition of you and your family. Probably I have been the instrumentality of your misfortunes. In my last moments I will think of the many favors you have done me, and if I had fifty kingdoms to present, you should have them all. But alas! I am poor and my fate is sealed. I would like to give you some advice but I fear you may think me presumptuous. What I would say is this: That you had better send the girls to San Francisco to the Sisters of Charity. There they will be educated and taken care of. Tell all the girls farewell! Tell them to be good girls and to be very careful to whom they pledge themselves for life. All the money I have is ten dollars, which I have given to Mr. Chism for Sarah. If you ever see Edward S., tell him my fate. I must come to a close, for the hounds are thirsting for my blood. Goodbye forever.

Thos. J. Bell

Dear Mother:

As I am about to make my exit to another country, I take this opportunity to write you a few lines. Probably you may never hear from me again. If not, I hope we may meet again where parting is no more.

*In my prodigal career in this country I have always rec-
ollected your fond admonitions, and if I had lived up to
them probably I would not have been in my present condition; but, dear mother, though my fate has been a cruel one,
yet I have no one to blame but myself. Give my respects to all
my old and youthful friends. Tell them to beware of bad as-
sociations and never to enter into any gambling saloons, for
that has been my ruin.*

*If my old Grandmother is living, remember me to her.
With these remarks, I bid you farewell forever.*

Your only boy,
Tom

[To the mob] *"Boys, I am only twenty-six years of age. "*

LUCKY BILL THORRINGTON (Thornton)
[Near Genoa, Nevada, June 19, 1858]

Found guilty of involvement in a murder and taken immediately
to be hanged, he did not want to be hanged from the slaughter
apparatus, a convenience vigilantes often used.

"If they want to hang me, I'm no hog."

[Singing] *The Last Rose of Summer.*

WILLIAM EDWARDS, Cattle Thief
[Honey Lake, Nevada, June 20, 1858]

Implicated in the same murder as Lucky Bill, he was given a vigilante trial and hanged.

*"I deserve what I'm getting...I helped kill Gordier...
But don't bury me away from all my friends.
Plant me in the upper valley, somewhere
between Streshly's cabin and mine...."*

BOB AUGUSTINE, Outlaw
[San Antonio, Texas, 1861]

Having gone on a troublemaking spree, he was grabbed by a Mexican mob during his trial, taken to Military Plaza, and lynched.

"Please don't hang me out of consideration for my mother. What will she think when she hears her Bob was strung up on a rope? Please, please, don't hang me—shoot me! I'll stand up like a man! Please!"

ANDREW WOOD, Outlaw
[Los Angeles, California, November 21, 1863]

Taken with other gang members, the young man showed his pluck on the vigilantes' makeshift gallows.

"I'm going to die a game hen-chicken!"

WILLIAM BUCKLEY, Outlaw Gang Member
[Aurora, Nevada, February 9, 1864]

Named as murderers, he and three others were hanged by vigilantes.

"Gentlemen, I do not stand here before you to say I am innocent. Daly and I are guilty. But there are two innocent men on the scaffold: McDowell and Masterson. I deserve to be punished and I die a brave man. Adieu, boys. I wish you well. All of you must come to my wake in John Daly's cabin tonight. Be sure of this. Goodbye. God bless."

JOHN DALY, Gang Leader
[Aurora, Nevada, February 9, 1864]

Hired gun, killer, he and his gang were finally taken by vigilantes and hanged.

[To a vigilante] *"You son of a bitch! If I had a six-shooter, I'd make you git!"*

[In response to Buckley's comments] *"Yes, Buckley and I did the deed. There are two innocent men on this scaffold. Are you going to hang them? Do you understand? I killed Johnson; Buckley and I did it. He was a damned Mormon thief. He was the means of killing my friend and I lived to die for him. Had I lived beyond this day I would have wiped out Johnson's whole generation!"*

JAMES MASTERSON, Outlaw Gang Member
[Aurora, Nevada, February 9, 1864]

Presumably one of the innocent ones, Masterson, no relation to the famous Bat Masterson, was hanged along with the rest of the gang.

"Gentlemen, I am innocent."

JOHN McDOWELL, Outlaw Gang Member
[Aurora, Nevada, February 9, 1864]

Pleading his innocence, "Three-Fingered Jack" was allowed to give a last hug to his girlfriend, who slipped him a defective derringer, which he put to his head, then hurled to the ground when it failed to fire.

"Goodbye, boys! The son of a bitch pistol has fooled me! So you want to murder me. Then I'll die like a tiger!"

JOSEPH "JACK" SLADE, Rancher
[Virginia City, Montana, March 10, 1864]

Alcoholic and quarrelsome, he was hoisted up on a storefront sign for causing more trouble than the miners wished to bear.

"My God! My God! Must I die like this? Oh my poor wife!"

ANONYMOUS HORSE THIEF #1
[Lacy's Grove, Nebraska, c. 1864]

Caught by vigilantes, he and his two partners were placed in a wagon and hanged from the same limb.

"This is pretty tough, but I've seen harder things than this."

ANONYMOUS HORSE THIEF #2
[Lacy's Grove, Nebraska, c. 1864]

Caught by the Nebraska vigilantes, he was given a chance to write a note to his mother.

"Dear Mother, our mischief for the past few years has come to an end. We got to stretch the rope. Don't grieve, Mother. Meet us in heaven."

L. H. JOSEPH MUSGROVE, Gang Leader
[Denver, Colorado, November 23, 1868]

Having for years led several gangs, including a gang of Indians, he was finally lynched, casually writing a letter while the vigilantes prepared his noose and then calmly flinging his cigarette at the crowd.

"I suppose you are going to hang me because I'm an Indian chief!... If you are bent upon murdering me, you will at least be men enough to permit me to write to my friends and tell them the shameful story of your conduct towards me."

My Dear Brother

I am to be hung to-day on false charges by a mob my children is in Napa Valley Cal—will you go and get them & take care of them for me godd Knows that I am innocent pray for me but I was here when the mob took me. Brother good by for Ever take care of my pore little children I remain your unfortunate Brother good by

L. H. Musgrove

Denver C. T.

My Dear Wife—Before this reaches you I will bee no more Mary I am as you know innocent of the charges made against me I do not know what they ar agoing to hang me for unless it is because I am acquainted with Ed Franklin— godd will protect you I hope Good by for ever as ever yours sell what I have and keep it.

L. H. Musgrove

[To the vigilantes] *"Go on with your work."*

[To someone's question as to where his gang was]*"I am sure I don't know, unless you are one of them."*

SANFORD S. C. DUGGAN, Outlaw
[Denver, Colorado, December 1, 1868]

Brought back to Denver for robbing the judge, he was taken from the marshal by a mob that cut short his whining.

"I killed the man in the mountains in self-defense and have been tried and acquitted. The man in the Black Hills was killed by another fellow. I never stole anything from anybody. I did assist in robbing Squire Brooks, but I was nearly out of money and had to do it or starve. I only had six or

*seven dollars, and could not get any any other way. I had to
do it or die. I have been a very bad man, but have done nothing to be hanged for. Spare my life—any other punishment.
Oh, my poor mother! It will kill her! Don't let it get to her.
Send for a Catholic minister."*

LEANDER MORTON, Convict
[Near Bishop Creek, California, September 30, 1871]

After being involved in a murder during an escape with twenty-
one others, he was captured and hanged, along with Moses
Black, while young Roberts was spared.

[To Black] *"Are you ready to die?...
Yes it is. Don't you hear them building the scaffold?"*

[To Roberts] *"We are to swing,
and I mean to have you hung with us if I can..."*

[To a vigilante] *"Take my coat collar from under the rope.
Don't hang a man with his collar under the rope..."*

[After a prayer] *"I am prepared to meet my God.
I don't know that there is a God."*

MOSES BLACK, Convict
[Near Bishop Creek, California, September 30, 1871]

In the same fix as Leander Morton, he replied, somewhat naively,
to Morton's query about being ready to die at the hands of the
lynch mob.

"No, this is not the crowd that will hang us."

GREEN MCCULLOUGH, Killer
[Texas, c. 1875]

After killing an innocent bystander, he began to protest to the lynch mob, then acquiesced.

*"Well, if I've got to be hung, I'm glad
I'm goin' to be hung by my friends."*

RICHARD BURNETT, Horse Thief
[Black Hills, February 26, 1876]

Caught in the act of horse theft, he was found guilty by a hastily organized "court" composed of prospectors and became the first man lynched in the Black Hills.

"I know I shot Pete Lambert, but he wanted to get the drop on me. I took his horse, and I may have taken a few others, but what I done I done when I was drunk. If I've got to swing, I will do it like a man, only give me the time to fix up matters afore I go."

CORNELIUS DONAHUE, Horse Thief
[Buffalo Gap, Dakota Territory, July 3(?), 1879]

In custody on his way to Rapid City, Donahue, alias "Lame Johnny" Hurley, was taken from the officer and hanged by a mob.

"Hang and be damned; you can't do it any too soon!"

SAM WOODRUFF, Murderer
[Golden, Colorado, December 27, 1879]

Taken to a railroad bridge to be hanged by vigilantes, he took too long to show his initiative and was shoved off, despite his last request.

> *"Gentlemen, you are hanging an innocent man, but I trust God will forgive you as I do.... May God have mercy on your souls.... May I say my prayers?... I have one last request to make. Permit me to jump off the bridge—don't push me to death."*

JOSEPH SEMINOLE, Murderer
[Golden, Colorado, December 27, 1879]

He was hanged on the same bridge and by the same vigilantes who hanged Sam Woodruff.

> *"Gentlemen, I have but little to say, and I address myself to those among you who may be erring ones. Beware of the first bad step. The after ones are not to be feared; it is the beginnings. But for my first evil break I would not be standing here tonight with this rope about my neck and death staring me in the face. In relation to this murder, gentlemen, we two are the guilty ones. We committed the crime. I have no excuse to offer, nothing to say...O, God Almighty, have mercy on my sinful soul; and as Thou hast shown Thy love and tenderness in times past, to weak and guilty ones, show such to me now. Guard, oh I pray Thee, my mother and brothers, and let not them follow in my footsteps or take my sinful path. Forgive me my transgressions, O God, and take me to Thee, sinful though I am."*

ANTHONY LOWE, Outlaw
[Las Vegas, New Mexico, February 7, 1880]

Being lynched for murder, Lowe, alias "James West," at first broke down, then regained his nerve.

"Boys, you are hanging a mighty good man.
Please button up my pants."

TOM JEFFERSON HOUSE, Outlaw
[Las Vegas, New Mexico, February 7, 1880]

After identifying himself and then giving moral support to his companion, Tom House, alias "Tom Henry," was shot by his victim's widow before he could be hanged.

"Boys, it's pretty rough to be hung, but I wish some one would write to my father and mother. I will stand the consequence and die like a man ... Jim, be still and die like a man ..."

[Shooting] *"Boys, for God's sake shoot me again! Shoot me in the head!"*

"BIG NOSE" GEORGE PARROTT, Outlaw
[Rawlins, Wyoming, March 22, 1881]

Sentenced to hang for murder, he attempted a jailbreak, his failure encouraging an inept mob whose first rope broke, only partially strangling him.

"I will jump off, boys, and break my neck."

CORNELIUS "CON" MURPHY, Horse Thief
[Near Helena, Montana, January 27, 1885]

After having escaped from the law several times in the past, the troublesome young horse thief, accompanied by his innocent younger brother, who was not harmed, was taken from lawmen by a vigilante group, transported to a railroad bridge, and hanged.

"Brother, kiss me."

BEN WHEELER, Outlaw
[Medicine Lodge, Kansas, April 30, 1884]

After Deputy Wheeler and Sheriff Brown of Caldwell, along with two others, attempted to rob the bank in Medicine Lodge, they were captured and lynched for the killing of bank teller George Geppert.

"Oh, men, spare my life. There's other fellows mixed up in this and I will tell you everything if only you will spare my life!"

WILLIAM SMITH, Outlaw
[Medicine Lodge, Kansas, April 30, 1884]

He was asked to say his last words before being lynched for the bank robbery and Geppert killing.

"What's the use anyway? So pull when you are ready."

IKE BARBER, Murderer
[Waverly, Iowa, June 8, 1883]

With his brother Bill, Barber was taken from the jail and lynched by a mob led by the brother of Deputy Shepard, who was killed by the Barbers nine months earlier.

"I'm going to tell you the truth. I know I'm going die in a short time. . . . We're horse thieves, not murderers. We never killed anyone until last Fall, and within the last two weeks."

JOHN WADE, Horse Thief
[Near Newport, Nebraska, November 10, 1883]

Taken from custody by a group of vigilantes, he was offered a drink and then killed.

"Yes, I'll take a drink with you."

BURT WILKINSON, Outlaw
[Silverton, Colorado, September 4, 1881]

Betrayed by Ike Stockton for the reward money, Wilkinson, killer of City Marshal D. R. Ogsbury, tried to accommodate the vigilantes who forced their way into his cell. He got up on a chair, assisted with the rope, and did not prolong the activities when asked if he had anything to say.

"Nothing, gentlemen. Adios!"

HARRY TUTTLE, Outlaw
[Spearfish, South Dakota, February 19, 1884]

Severely wounded in the gunfight which killed Deputy O'Hara, and dying in the Spearfish hospital, he was taken out and lynched to satisfy the desire for vengeance.

"Hurry up and get it over with."

THEODORE BAKER, Murderer
[Las Vegas, New Mexico, May 6, 1887]

Baker has the rare distinction of being hanged twice for the same crime, that of killing the husband of his lover. Two days after the crime, he was lynched and left for dead, but the sheriff arrived and cut him down. His description of this hanging, given to a newspaper reporter, might be representative of the last words of many hanging victims if the rope weren't so tight.

> *"I went with them, and at the jail door I began to curse them, when one of them put the muzzle of his pistol to my ear and said: 'Keep still or I'll put a bullet through you.' I knew him by his voice, and knew he would do it, and I kept still. A little further on we came to a telegraph pole. From the crossbar swung a new rope. On the end was a big slip-noose. They led me under the rope. I tried to stoop down and pull my boots off, as I had promised my folks not to die with my boots on, but before I could do it the noose was thrown over my head and I was jerked off my feet. My senses left me for a moment, and then I waked up in what seemed to be another world. As I recollect now, the sensation was that everything about me had been multiplied a great many times. It seemed that my five executioners had grown in number until there were thousands of them. I saw what seemed to be a multitude of animals of all shapes and sizes.*
>
> *Then things changed and I was in great pain. I became conscious that I was hanging by the neck, and that the knot*

of the rope had slipped under my chin. My hands were loosely tied, and I jerked them loose and tried to catch the rope above me. Somebody caught me by the feet just then and gave me a jerk. It seemed like a bright flash of lightning passed in front of my eyes. It was the brightest thing I ever saw. It was followed by a terrible pain up and down and across my back and I could feel my legs jerk and draw up. Then there was a blank, and I knew nothing more until eleven o'clock the next day."

[His real last words were uttered on a legal scaffold, a year and a half after the crime.]

"Gentlemen, I am sorry it ends this way. Let her go."

DANNY ARATA, Saloonkeeper
[Denver, Colorado, July 27, 1893]

After killing a customer because he didn't have the five cents to pay for his beer, the hot-headed Italian immigrant was taken from the jail by an enraged mob who tore his clothing for souvenirs, put a rope around his neck, asked him if he were guilty, and hoisted him to a cottonwood tree.

"Yes. Hurry up and be done with me."

JOHN J. HOOVER, Murderer
[Fairplay, Colorado, April, 28, 1880]

Charged with murder but found guilty of manslaughter, he received a reduced sentence, which aroused the vigilantes who broke into the courthouse and hanged him from a second-story window.

"Must I die like a dog?"

ELMER "KID" LEWIS, Outlaw
[Wichita Falls, Texas, February 25, 1896]

Having killed a man during a holdup, Kid Lewis was dragged from his cell and lynched.

> *"Boys, a man can't die only once. I'm not afraid.*
> *Besides, what's life without a friend?"*

CHARLES FRANCIS WOODARD
[Casper, Wyoming, March 28, 1902]

Sentenced to hang on March 28 for the murder of Sheriff Ricker, he was granted a stay of execution, only to be dragged from the jail by a mob that was not going to be denied its hanging.

> *"To my blessed little wife. Tell my dear little wife I love her dearly. Won't you tell her that, boys? I pray that you have the paper print it. God forgive me for my sins. I pray for myself, I pray for all of you and I pray for Charlie Ricker. I never had a grudge against him in God's world. I never meant to shoot him ... Don't choke me, boys. For God's sake, you are choking me ... God have mercy on me and save me, and I pray for my blessed dear wife ... Don't choke me to death, boys ... I did not shoot Charlie Ricker on purpose. Lord have mercy on me and my little wife. Don't choke me, boys. Oh—"*

TROUBLEMAKERS

JAMES HILL
[Denver, Colorado, November 25, 1860]

Hill was shot by Charley Harrison after Harrison reprimanded Hill for calling Harrison's bartender a son of a bitch.

"I'll call him as I please, and you ain't no better ..."

WILLIAM "BILLY" PAGE
[Lewiston, Idaho Territory, December 25, 1866]

Out of jealousy over a whore, Page, the main witness in the Magruder murder trial two years earlier, provoked a man who, before shooting, threatened him.

"You will, oh you son of a bitch!"

JARRETT FISHER, Outlaw
[Evansville, Arkansas, January 2, 1869]

Having earlier won a horse and saddle from young Maurice Shannon in a poker game, and having been told by Shannon's father that the debt would not be paid because Maurice was too young to be playing poker, Fisher threatened Maurice by sticking his gun into the boy's mouth but was gunned down by Maurice's older brother, who entered the saloon.

"Go home and tell your Daddy that we expect to have that money by noon tomorrow or we will take it out of your hide!"

HAYS TAYLOR, Outlaw
[Karnes County, Texas, August 23, 1869]

Caught in a postwar cleanup of outlaw bands, he charged the soldiers who apparently had captured his father.

"I will not leave my father there! I will go to him!"

WILLIAM McWATERS, Convict
[Nebraska State Penitentiary, Lincoln, Nebraska, May 26, 1875]

Considered by the guards to be dangerous because of a previous escape attempt, he was shot down when he picked up two large rocks and uttered words that the guard thought were directed at him.

"I'll fix that son of a bitch now!"

BILL GALLAGHER, Outlaw
[Near Fort Sumner, New Mexico, 1876]

In a quarrel with tough rancher John Slaughter, he wildly charged on horseback and was coolly shot down by Slaughter. In his last moments, he did some philosophical self-analysis.

"I needed killing twenty years ago, anyway."

SOSTENES L'ARCHEVEQUE, Outlaw
[Texas Panhandle, summer 1876]

Having become too violent and troublesome even for his friends, he was invited to a friend's house for a meal, ambushed, stabbed, and shot.

"You pull that knife out of my back,
and I'll kill every one of you!"

JOHN D. MASSINGALE, Private
[Bismarck, Dakota Territory, December 25, 1876]

Celebrating Christmas in a bordello, the drunken soldier antagonized Pete Bannigan, the owner, by insisting on a fight.

"I can whip any damn son of a bitch for ten dollars!"

[To Bannigan] *"You pimping son of a bitch, get your revolver! I will kill you before I leave this house! I am a fighting son of a bitch from Scranton!"*

[After a struggle] *"I wonder where he has gone now?"*

[Gunshot] *"Oh, my God!"*

"WHISKEY JIM" GREATHOUSE, Rustler
[San Mateo Mountains, December 1881]

Having recently rustled and sold some horses, he and his partners realized, a moment too late, that the two men they were now traveling with were just waiting for an unguarded moment to arrest them.

"I know your racket, but it won't work!"

THOMAS STEELE, Mine Agent
[Eagle City, Idaho, June 19, 1884]

When his companion, a drunk prostitute, fell in the street and refused to get up, Steele began slapping her. Hearing a voice tell him not to hurt her, Steele turned and mistakenly confronted bystander Dan Ferguson, Wyatt Earp's business partner. Approaching Ferguson, Steele demanded,

"Now what have you got to do with this?"

Before Ferguson could explain, Steele hit him on the temple with a revolver and said,

"Damn you! I'll fix you!"

Ferguson drew his gun, and in the ensuing gunfight, Steele was killed.

CHARLES W. WILSON, Troublemaker
[Hot Sulphur Springs, Colorado, December 9, 1884]

Having terrorized the town for a week, the teen-aged badman known as "Texas Charley" was assassinated on the main street by a dozen or so "unknown" citizens whose first bullets were near misses.

"Seems to be getting pretty warm around here."

CHARLES P. STANTON
[Stanton, Arizona, November 13, 1886]

Involved in years of behind-the-scenes criminal activity, he was attacked and shot in his store one dark night by the brothers of Froilana Lucero, whose honor they were defending.

"I'm killed! Blow out the light!"

SAMUEL ROHN
[San Diego, California, November 1887]

While sleeping on the steps of a building in the red-light district, he was awakened by Constable Gedney, who, attempting to identify the sleeper, held a match close to Rohn's face. Startled, Rohn leapt up and was ordered by Gedney to stay back or he would be shot.

"Shoot if you dare!"

A. KOHLER, Con Man
[Green River, Utah, 1891 or early 1892]

After antagonizing Cass Hite by forming a mining company with a name similar to Hite's successful company, Kohler, sitting on the porch of the Gammage Hotel, rifle in his lap, missed his mark when he responded to Hite's inquiry as to what the problem might be.

"I'll show you!"

RICE BROWN, Cowboy
[Trinidad, Colorado, December 30, 1881]

Ordered out of town by deputies, Brown and his partner, after mounting their horses, lingered long enough to curse the officers but were interrupted by Sheriff Kreeger, who grabbed the reins, ordered the cowboys down, and drew Brown's fire. Kreeger shot Brown's horse, then shot three times into Brown, who stumbled away still snapping his empty pistol.

"Let go of that horse or I'll kill you!"

"DUTCH" FRED HIHN, Ex-City Marshal
[Boise, Idaho, August 31, 1881]

Drunk and belligerent, Hihn demanded the attentions of his favorite whore, ignoring the attempts of others to stop him, until he was shot by a protective patron.

"I don't care. I can go and burst the door and drag the pimpy son of a bitch and her, too. No shenanigan with me tonight. I will do it ... No damn son of a bitch stops me from bursting no door ... You damned son of a bitch, you have shot me."

SPOTTED HORSE, Pawnee Indian
[Caldwell, Kansas, May 14, 1883]

After wandering in the town, perhaps drunk, begging, and threatening some residents, he was fired upon, perhaps hastily, by Sheriff Henry Brown.

"Hold on, John, wait, me get my gun."

SAM STARR, Outlaw
[Near Whitefield, Indian Territory, December 18, 1886]

At a dance, recognizing a lawman who had attempted to arrest him three months earlier, the drunk Starr drew his gun to start the gunfight in which both were killed.

"You are the son of a bitch who shot me and killed my horse that day in the cornfield!"

LIBRADO PUEBLA, Convict
[Yuma Prison, Yuma, Arizona, late October, 1887]

Wounded four times in a desperate escape attempt in which he attacked Superintendent Gates, he lingered for half an hour before realizing that death was near.

"Well, what do I care? Adios."

WASH MIDDLETON, Fugitive
[Parthenon, Arkansas, July 4, 1888]

Wanted for a three-year-old killing, he was surprised during the Independence Day celebrations by private detective John Holt, who, gun drawn, informed Middleton that he was under arrest.

"I don't know that I am!"

JACK THOMAS, Rancher
[Duchesne Strip, Utah, early May, 1889]

The Duchesne Strip, near Fort Duchesne, which was manned by black troops, was an isolated and virtually lawless strip of land set aside by the federal government for mining interests. In this free-wheeling atmosphere, the drunk Thomas interfered in an argument between a white man and a black soldier, the soldier winning the gun battle.

"Like hell! You black son of a bitch! I will kill you!"

ANONYMOUS SHEEPHERDER
[Feild Sheep Ranch, Burnet County, Texas, 1889]

Having reluctantly taken a job herding sheep and then failing to watch them properly, the cowboy, when fired, was roused to violence, shooting at but missing his boss, Andy Feild, whose aim was perfect.

"You son of a bitch! You've fired your last man!"

WILLIAM KINGEN, Escaped Convict
[Near Cheyenne, Wyoming, January 3, 1891]

On the run with two other convicts, he and Charley Miller, exhausted, lay down and curled up, caught by the bitter cold. Kingen froze to death.

"Oh, I'm so cold, Charley; so awful cold!"

JAMES SMITH
[San Diego, California, April 1895]

Because of an altercation with a woman, he became the object of a police search and, after being found sitting in a horse stall, he was shot when he attacked with a knife the constable, who informed him that he had an arrest warrant for Smith.

"You have, you god damned son of a bitch!"

WILLIAM ALLEN, Cowboy
[Culbertson, Montana, December 8, 1894]

Reluctant to return a borrowed saddle to its owner, Charles Seppich, Allen seemed finally to give in. He then drew his revolver, permanently losing possession of the saddle.

"There's your saddle. Take it!"

JACK SMITH, Outlaw
[Altman, Colorado, May 14, 1895]

Generally a thorn in the side of the authorities, he was gunned down by Marshal Kelley but lived for a day, long enough to be baptized before becoming delirious.

"Don't you hear that shooting? The deputies are advancing and we must head 'em off!"

TRAIN ROBBERS

OSCAR BROWN, Outlaw
[Wheatland, California, March 30, 1895]

Shot while attempting a train robbery, he was abandoned by his partner.

"Don't leave me, Bill! Take me with you!"

DAN MCCALL, Train Robber
[Near Tulare, California, March 19, 1896]

Betrayed by his partner, who slipped away to warn officers, McCall attempted a holdup on a moving train, unaware that two officers were aboard. His final words were probably directed to his partner, who McCall thought was somewhere on the train.

"Throw up your hands, you damned sons of bitches!"

[Gunshots.] *"Why don't you shoot? Why don't you shoot?"*

COLE YOUNG, Train Robber
[Watering station near Albuquerque, New Mexico, October 2, 1896]

In an attempted train robbery, the twenty-five-year-old bandit was hit by a shotgun blast, stumbled into the dark, and bled to death as his two companions called for him to come.

"I can't come. I am done for."

BEN KILPATRICK, Outlaw
[Near Sanderson, Texas, March 13, 1912]

During a train holdup, he uttered his last words just before being smashed over the head with an ice hammer in the hands of express messenger Truesdale, who, being ordered to come along, stalled for time by asking if he could get his coat.

"Sure. Hell, wear your hat too."

OLE BECK, Outlaw
[Near Sanderson, Texas, March 13, 1912]

Responding to shots which he assumed were fired by his partner Ben Kilpatrick, who was called "Frank" during the train robbery, he stuck his head into the express car, where express messenger Truesdale was waiting for him with Kilpatrick's gun.

"Frank, are you in there?"

MORE VIGILANTE ACTION

JOHN LARN, Rustler
[Albany, Texas, June 24, 1878]

Ex-sheriff turned rustler, he was arrested, chained, and, in the middle of the night, shot by eleven masked men who subdued his guard but not his courage.

"If you'll turn me loose and give me a forty-five, I'll fight your whole outfit. Go ahead, I'll take my medicine."

JAMES MARTIN "MART" HORRELL
[Meridian, Texas, December 15, 1878]

In jail on charges of aiding and abetting a murder, he and his brother Tom, two of the violent Horrell brothers, were shot down in their cell by a lynch mob.

"Shoot, damn you, I can stand it!"

AL SCHWARTZ, Rancher
[Prineville, Oregon, late December, 1882]

Having been critical of the area's vigilantes, and perhaps suspected of being a horse thief, he sat down by a window, through which he was shot.

"Why is that window up? It's cold."

WILLIAM EDENS, Farmer
[Near Oldfield, Missouri, March 11, 1887]

Having antagonized the local vigilante group known as the Bald Knobbers, he was assassinated when the men broke into his house, ordered him to raise his hands, then blasted him with shotguns.

"I have them up. I have both of them up."

LEWELLYN "EPP" MARLOW
[Near Graham, Texas, January 19, 1889]

While the four Marlow brothers, lawfully chained together, were being transported at night to avoid a mob that followed and attacked, he was shot and, on the ground, responded to his brother's question.

"No—I can never get up anymore."

FRANK HARMISON
[Near Graham, Texas, January 19, 1889]

In one of the West's most famous gunfights, he and others of the mob were in retreat but, when the chained and wounded Marlows accused them of cowardice, he reversed direction, prompting a mob member to ask where he was going.

"Back to see it out!"

A. J. MAUPIN, Rustler
[Springview, Nebraska, July 13, 1889]

When the vigilantes failed to break into the jail, they came around to the window and shot Maupin, who, perhaps not wanting to be left seriously wounded, stepped up to the window bars.

"Do your best, men."

J. P. WALTERS, Murderer
[Basin, Wyoming, September 1903]

When a lynch mob broke into the jail and began using a sledgehammer to break the locks on the steel cage, he lit a candle, came forward, and offered himself to their rifles.

"Boys, no use to break things. If you want me, here I am."

BRUCE COOPER, Rancher
[NH Ranch, near Aragon, New Mexico, May 11, 1918]

When his Hispanic neighbors, tired of the larcenous Coopers, caught them in the act of butchering a stolen cow, Cooper reached for his rifle and tried to keep the evidence from view.

"You dirty Mexican half-breeds, if you come in here, I'll kill you!"

122

FIRING-SQUAD JUSTICE

JOHN DOYLE LEE, Mormon Leader
[Mountain Meadows, Utah, March 23, 1877]

Convicted of murder for his part in the Mountain Meadows massacre twenty years earlier, Lee chose death by a firing squad and was executed on the site of the killings after making a speech denouncing the Mormon Church, which he felt he had been protecting when he and others massacred a wagon-train of immigrants.

"I have but little to say this morning. Of course I feel that I am upon the brink of eternity; and the solemnities of eternity should rest upon my mind at the present. I have made out—or have endeavored to do so—a manuscript, abridging the history of my life. This is to be published. In it I have given my views and feelings with regard to these things.

I feel resigned to my fate. I feel as calm as a summer morn, and I have done nothing intentionally wrong. My conscience is clear before God and man. I am ready to meet my Redeemer and those that have gone before me, behind the vail.

I am not an infidel. I have not denied God and his mercies.

I am a strong believer in these things. Most I regret is parting with my family; many of them are unprotected and will be left fatherless. When I speak of these things they touch a tender chord within me. I declare my innocence of ever doing anything designedly wrong in all this affair. I used my utmost endeavors to save those people.

I would have given worlds, were they at my command, if I could have averted that calamity, but I could not do it. It went on.

It seems I have to be made a victim—a victim must be had, and I am the victim. I am sacrificed to satisfy the feelings—the vindictive feelings, or in other words, am used to gratify parties.

I am ready to die. I trust in God. I have no fear. Death has no terror.

Not a particle of mercy have I asked of the court, the world, or officials to spare my life.

I do not fear death, I shall never go to a worse place than I am now in.

I have said to my family, and I will say it today, that the Government of the United States sacrifices their best friend. That is saying a great deal, but it is true—it is so.

I am a true believer in the gospel of Jesus Christ. I do not believe everything that is now being taught and practiced by Brigham Young. I do not care who hears it. It is my last word—it is so. I believe he is leading the people astray, downward to destruction. But I believe in the gospel that was taught in its purity by Joseph Smith, in former days. I have my reasons for it.

I studied to make this man's will my pleasure for thirty years. See, now, what I have come to this day!

I have been sacrificed in a cowardly, dastardly manner. I cannot help it. It is my last word—it is so.

Evidence has been brought against me which is as false as the hinges of hell, and this evidence was wanted to sacrifice me. Sacrifice a man that has waited upon them, that has wandered and endured with them in the days of adversity, true from the beginnings of the Church! And I am now

124

singled out and am sacrificed in this manner! What confidence can I have in such a man! I have none, and I don't think my Father in heaven has any.

Still, there are thousands of people in this Church that are honorable and good-hearted friends, and some of whom are near to my heart. There is a kind of living, magnetic influence which has come over the people, and I cannot compare it to anything else than the reptile that enamors its prey, till it captivates it, paralyzes it, and rushes it into the jaws of death. I cannot compare it to anything else. It is so, I know it, I am satisfied of it.

I regret leaving my family; they are near and dear to me. These are things which touch my sympathy, even when I think of those poor orphaned children.

I declare I did nothing designedly wrong in this unfortunate affair. I did everything in my power to save that people, but I am the one that must suffer.

Having said this, I feel resigned. I ask the Lord, my God, if my labors are done, to receive my spirit."

[To the executioners] *"Center my heart, boys. Don't mangle my body!"*

CHARLES HOWARD, Lawyer
[San Elizario, Texas, December 17, 1877]

After having tried to control the salt beds near El Paso and angering the Mexican population, he was eventually captured and put in front of a firing squad. Trying to reason with the Mexicans, he failed to make them understand that they were killing not only him, but themselves and their community as well.

"Three hundred men—
You are going to kill three hundred men ... Fire."

JOHN ATKINSON, Merchant
[San Elizario, Texas, December 17, 1877]

Having befriended Charles Howard, he was caught up in the vengeance of the Mexican mob and put in front of a firing squad, whose first volley hit below the heart and left him still standing.

"Then let me die with honor. I will give the word ... When I give the word, fire at my heart ... Higher! Mas arriba, cabrones!"

SILAN LEWIS, Choctaw Indian
[Brown's Prairie, Choctaw Nation, November 5, 1894]

Sentenced to death by a Choctaw court and released on his own recognizance until the execution date, he showed up on time and chose a boyhood friend to fire the fatal shot.

"Want boy to have pony and rifle..."

[In Choctaw] *"We will be together again, somewhere, sometime ... Time up. Choctaw law say Silan Lewis must be shot. Want Lyman Pusley do it ... Yes ..."* [Choctaw prayer].

GUNFIGHTERS

ANONYMOUS GUNFIGHTER
[Near Lehi, Utah, c. 1850]

Confronting the seemingly invincible longhaired gunfighter Orrin Porter Rockwell, known as the "Mormon Avenging Angel," the anonymous young gunfighter was distracted by Rockwell just long enough for Rockwell to draw and fire.

"I heard that you can't be killed because of your hair. You have seen your last minute on earth. I've ridden miles to kill you!"

JOHN VEDDER, Gambler
[Nevada City, California, 1857]

Desperate, jealous, and confused, Vedder, revolver in hand, went to the Hotel de Paris, where his estranged wife was being protected from further domestic violence by Sheriff Henry Plummer. The sheriff was forced to shoot the aggressive Vedder.

"Your time is come!"

JIM WEBSTER, Fugitive
[Northern California, late 1857]

He quarreled with one of his men and ordered him to leave camp. Next morning, he raised his rifle upon seeing the man, who not only did not leave the camp, but also managed, during the night, to remove the shells from Webster's rifle.

"So, you didn't go!"

WILLIAM WILLOUGHBY
[Florence, Idaho, January 2, 1863]

Helping his friend Cherokee Bob settle a quarrel that began on New Year's Eve, Willoughby was killed in the ensuing gunfight, riddled with sixteen gunshot wounds.

"For God's sake, don't shoot anymore. I'm dying now."

HENRY J. TALBOT, Gambler/Saloon Owner
[Florence, Idaho, January 5, 1863]

Mortally wounded in a gunfight with another saloon owner Jacob Williams and Williams' friend Rube Robbins, Henry "Cherokee Bob" Talbot lingered for several days, erroneously believing that he had killed Williams, and, at one point, commenting on his antagonists' gunfighting skills with cap-and-ball revolvers.

"They are both brave men, but with this difference; Jakey always steps aside to get clear of the smoke of his revolver, while Rube pushes through it and keeps on coming, getting nearer his adversary with each shot."

[Near death] *"Tell my brother I have killed my man and gone on a long hunt."*

JACK CLEVELAND
[Bannack, Montana, January 14, 1863]

After a falling-out and a shootout with Henry Plummer, the dying Cleveland was asked for information concerning his trouble with Plummer, but he refused to incriminate his adversary.

*"It makes no difference to you. Poor Jack has got no friends.
He has got it, and I guess he can stand it. "*

JOHN KEENE, Murderer
[Helena, Montana, fall 1864]

Having shot down his enemy, gambler Harry Slater, Keene was given a hasty trial and quickly hanged.

"What I have done to Slater I have done willingly. He punished me severely. Honor compelled me to do what I have done. He run me from town to town. I tried to shun him here, but he saw me—called me a ———, and smacked me in the face. I did not want any trouble with him. My honor compelled me to do what I have done. I am here, and must die, and if I was to live till tomorrow, I would do the same thing again. I am ready. Jerk the cart as soon as you please."

JAMES BUTLER "WILD BILL" HICKOK
[Deadwood, Dakota Territory, August 2, 1876]

He wasn't having any luck even before he drew his final poker hand, aces and eights, and was shot in the back of the head by Jack McCall.

"The old duffer—he broke me on the hand."

MORGAN COURTNEY, Mine Superintendent
[Pioche, Nevada, August 1, 1873]

The formidable gunfighter was ambushed as he left a saloon, shot five times by gambler George McKinney, with whom he had an ongoing dispute, partially over the attentions of prostitute Georgiana Syphers.

> *"McKinney shot me. He shot me in the back—I started to run away in order to defend myself, but he shot so fast."* [Vomits blood.] *"Frank Cleveland gave him the pistol— Georgie Syphers told me. I did not shoot McKinney at all. I did not get my pistol out until he shot six shots."*

JOEL COLLINS, Train Robber
[Near Buffalo Station, Kansas, October 26, 1877]

Halted by a sheriff and ten soldiers on suspicion of robbing a train with the Sam Bass gang, he and Bill Heffridge at first protested their innocence, then went down fighting.

> *"Pard, if we are to die, we might as well die game."*

LEANDRO URIETA
[La Mesilla, New Mexico, November 2, 1877]

Before being killed by the sheriff, he took a rifle and, probably drunk and seeking revenge for a friend who had just been gunned down, began shooting at passersby until halted by a deputy, at whom he also shot.

> *"You're the one I wanted anyway!"*

"WILD" BILL LONGLEY, Gunfighter
[Giddings, Texas, October 11, 1878]

One of the most dangerous men of the West, Longley finally went to the shaky gallows for the murder of one of his thirty-two victims, a hanging watched by some ten thousand spectators.

[Reacting to the creaking gallows as he stepped up] *"Look out there. Let's don't get crippled up before the show is over ... I have got to die. I see a good many enemies around me and mighty few friends. I hope to God you will forgive me. I will you. I hate to die, of course; any man hates to die, but I have learned this by taking the lives of men who loved life as well as I do. If I have any friends here, I hope they will do nothing to avenge my death. If they want to avenge my death, let them pray for me. I deserve this fate. It is a debt I owe for my wild reckless life. When it is paid it will all be over. I hope you will forgive me. I forgive you. Whether you do or not, may God forgive me. I have nothing more to say. Goodbye everybody."*

LEVI RICHARDSON, Freighter
[Dodge City, Kansas, April 5, 1879]

In the famous Long Branch Saloon, he taunted gambler Frank Loving, outdrew him, and quickly fanned five shots, all of which missed. Loving carefully shot him to death.

"Why don't you fight?"

JOE GRANT

[Fort Sumner, New Mexico, January 10, 1880]

During an evening of drinking, he went to some trouble to pick a fight with Billy the Kid, who had earlier set Grant's gun so that the trigger would fall on an empty chamber.

"That's a lie!"

MIKE MEAGHER, Former Lawman

[Caldwell, Kansas, December 17, 1881]

He was shot in a gunfight with Texan Jim Talbot.

"Tell my wife I have got it at last."

JOHN KING FISHER, Gunman

[San Antonio, Texas, March 11, 1884]

Before he and gunman Ben Thompson were gunned down by hidden assassins in the Vaudeville Theatre, he tried to patch up the enmity between Thompson and his enemies.

"I want you and Thompson to be friends. You are both friends to me and I want you to shake hands like gentlemen."

JAMES W. "SIX SHOOTER" SMITH, Outlaw

[Cibolo Station, Texas, June 23, 1882]

Shot by pursuers for the killing of Marshal Johnson of Laredo, he died the next day, addressing his last words to some woman in his past.

"Well, Molly, it's all over now."

TIMOTHY ISAIAH "LONGHAIR JIM" COURTRIGHT
[Fort Worth, Texas, February 8, 1887]

Former city marshal, long-time gunfighter, he continued shaking down the gamblers until he ran into fearless gambler/gunfighter Luke Short in one of the West's most famous gunfights.

"Don't you pull a gun on me!"

[To Officer Fulford] *"Ful, they've got me."*

ED S. FUNK, Hired Gun
[Kirbyville, Missouri, July 4, 1889]

As the influence of the Bald Knobbers began to wane, Funk was hired to kill Billy Miles, who, when he was found at the Independence Day celebrations, replied in the affirmative to Funk's questions.

"Is your name Miles? Bill Miles? Have you a gun?"

[Miles: "Do you have one?"]

"Yes, and I'll shoot your brains out!"

PAT GARRETT, Rancher/Former Lawman
[Near Organ, New Mexico, February 29, 1908]

Possibly the victim of a conspiracy, Garrett, before being shot in the back of the head on the way to Las Cruces, got down from the wagon to urinate, interrupting his ongoing argument with Wayne Brazel, who suggested he might keep the ranch lease which Garrett wanted back.

"Well, damn you. If I don't get you off one way, I will another."

JEFF KIDDER, Sergeant, Arizona Rangers
[Naco, Mexico, April 5, 1908]

While on an unofficial visit to the cantinas on the Mexican side of Naco, he was gutshot by Mexican police after a misunderstanding with a Mexican prostitute. Failing to re-cross the border, he was beaten and thrown in jail, then removed to a private home, where, after visits by a doctor and a reporter from Bisbee, he died, thirty hours after the gunfight.

"I had not had a chance to move when two Mexican police came through the doorway with their six-shooters drawn, and one fired, hitting me. I fell and was dazed, but knew that my only chance was to fight while I had cartridges left. I drew my own six-shooter while sitting on the floor and opened fire. I believe I wounded both of the men, and they went down helpless. I was very weak.

. . . Suddenly firing opened up in front of me, and I saw a number of men between me and the line armed with Winchesters. They were directing their fire directly at me . . .

When I got to the fence, I put the last six cartridges I had into my gun. During all this time these men were firing at me . . . I saved my fire until one of their number came within range and I shot him. I then fired until my gun was empty. When my last cartridge was gone I yelled to them that I was all in and told them to come and get me . . .

If anybody had told me that one human being could be as brutal to another as they were to me I would not have believed it. I could scarcely stand, but one of this crowd . . .struck me over the head with his six-shooter and I fell. Between them they dragged me on the ground for about fifty yards, and then seemingly tired of their exertions stopped and beat me over the head with a six-shooter. They finally dragged me to the jail and threw me in there . . .

I know that a great many people think I am quick-tempered. I did not precipitate this trouble, and never drew my gun until I was wounded and on the floor of that house . . .

If I am fatally wounded, I can die with the knowledge that I did my best in a hard situation ...

You know, Jack, that I would not lie to you. I know that I am done for ... They got me, but if my ammunition had not given out, I might have served them the same way."

I SHOT THE LAW

JAMES BARTON, Sheriff
[Near San Juan, California, late January, 1857]

In an exchange of gunfire with outlaws, he fell after replying to his adversary's claim: "I've got you now!"

"I reckon I have got you too!"

WILLIAM C. STODDARD, Lawyer
[Near Sacramento, California, July 26, 1860]

Helping transport murder suspect William Wells by wagon, Stoddard and two guards, Armstrong and Wharton, relaxed their vigilance, Armstrong falling asleep near the prisoner, who snatched one of Armstrong's revolvers as Armstrong was roused from sleep. Wells escaped after killing the three guards.

"We are near Sacramento. You better wake up Armstrong."

SUMNER "OLD PINK" PINKHAM, Deputy U.S. Marshal
[Warm Springs, Idaho, July 13, 1865]

Ferd Patterson, having been previously beaten up by Pinkham, challenged him by saying, "Draw, will you?"

"I will!"

CHAUNCEY WHITNEY, Sheriff
[Ellsworth, Kansas, August 15, 1873]

Attempting to settle a quarrel that involved his friend Ben Thompson, he was struck by the blast from a shotgun fired by drunk Billy Thompson.

*"He did not intend to do it. It was an accident.
Send for my family."*

CHARLEY WEBB, Deputy Sheriff
[Comanche, Texas, May 26, 1874]

Before shooting—but only wounding—dangerous John Wesley Hardin, he tried to put him off guard by replying to Hardin's blunt question of a warrant.

"No, I don't have any warrant for you, Wes."

ED MASTERSON, City Marshal
[Dodge City, Kansas, April 9, 1878]

Shot on the street while trying to disarm two cowboys, his shirt smoldering from the muzzle blast, the brother of the famous Bat Masterson stumbled into Hoover's saloon and fell beside the bartender.

"George, I'm shot."

ELLIS GRIMES, Deputy Sheriff
[Round Rock, Texas, July 19, 1878]

Seeing members of the Sam Bass gang enter a store, one with a revolver under his coat, he and another deputy died in the swift response to his question.

"You packin' a gun?"

JOHN USSHER, Provincial Constable
[Near Government Camp, British Columbia, December 8, 1879]

Attempting, with others, to arrest the McLean brothers and Alexander Hare for horse theft, he was only partially right—they knifed him before shooting him.

"They'll never fire a shot. Come on. I'll take the lead."

F. MARION SHEPARD, Deputy
[Railroad camp, near Wadena, Iowa, September 7, 1882]

Possibly unaware that the Barber brothers were desperate murderers and not merely horse thieves, Shepard was shot without hesitation as he approached them.

"Throw up your arms. You are my prisoners!"

JACK O'HARA, Deputy
[Stoneville, Montana, February 14, 1884]

He was shot while he and another deputy tried to arrest a gang of outlaws.

*"Fred, I stayed with you as long as I could;
give them the best you have."*

SAMUEL C. TOWNSEND, Police Officer
[Leadville, Colorado, March 28, 1882]

Following an argument that led to a scuffle, he was shot by T. C. Early and taken to a drugstore where, surrounded by his wife Alice and family, he bled to death while he responded to questions.

"Please, don't bother me ... Oh, you don't know how much misery I'm in...Take care of the boy, George ... God bless you, Allie."

WILL FIELDS, Captain, Indian Police
[Near Eufala, Creek Nation, April 10, 1887]

He attempted to arrest Jim Cunnieus, who shot him.

"Jim, I've got a writ for you; throw down your gun!"

FRANK DALTON, Deputy U.S. Marshal
[Near Fort Smith, Arkansas, November 27, 1887]

Attempting to arrest a horse thief named Dave Smith, Dalton, older brother of the soon-to-be infamous Dalton brothers, was mortally wounded in the chest by Smith and then finished off by William Towerly, who callously disregarded Dalton's last words.

"Please don't fire. I'm preparing to die."

JOHN BURNS, Sheriff
[Near Custer City, South Dakota, July 11, 1889]

Sent to arrest Johnny Lehman, the sheriff, seeing Lehman armed and obviously upset, decided to withdraw, but Lehman raised his rifle and fired.

"Don't shoot, John. We are leaving!"

GEORGE THORNTON, Deputy
[Creek Nation, October 29, 1891]

During an attempt to apprehend a fugitive, he was shot in the side.

"Oh, I'm sick."

FLOYD WILSON, Lawman
[Lenapah, Oklahoma, December 14, 1892]

When trying to arrest Henry Starr, his Winchester jammed. Starr's weapon worked more efficiently.

"Hold up! I have a warrant for you!"

FRANK JONES, Texas Ranger Captain
[Tres Jacales, Mexico, June 30, 1893]

After a Mexican rustler's bullet hit him in the leg and knocked him from the saddle, he took another bullet in the chest just after a Ranger asked him if he were hurt.

"Yes, shot all to pieces ... Boys, I am killed."

WILLIAM KELLY, Deputy
[Near Trinidad, Colorado, June 1897]

Approaching the hideout of outlaws who opened fire, killing his partner and wounding him, he threw down his weapons and tried to surrender to the Spanish-speaking vaqueros.

"Not to kill; not to kill."

EDWARD J. FARR, Sheriff
[Near Cimarron, New Mexico, July 16, 1899]

In a shootout with the "Black Jack" Ketchum gang, he received a second wound to the chest.

"I'm done for."

CARLOS TAFOLLA, Arizona Ranger
[Near St. Johns, Arizona, October 8, 1901]

Having been a part of the newly formed Arizona Rangers for less than a month, he lay mortally wounded, shot while attempting to arrest outlaws.

"Give this dollar to my wife. It, and the month's wages coming to me, will be all she'll ever have."

BILLY STILES, Outlaw
[Riley Ranch, Humboldt County, Nevada, December 5, 1908]

Once a lawman, Stiles, though a wanted man, was at the time of his death again acting as a lawman under the assumed name of William Larkin. He was serving civil papers when he was unexpectedly shot.

"Oh, Jesus Christ."

EDGAR WILLIAMS, Town Marshal
[Rosebud, Texas, December 22, 1909]

Shot in the stomach while trying to arrest Coke Mills, who was subsequently lynched in the town's bell tower, Williams lingered for two days before succumbing to his wounds.

"I especially regret having been shot by a Negro."

141

ALEXANDER KINDNESS, Constable
[Near Clinton, British Columbia, May 3, 1912]

As Provincial Police Constable Kindness and his posse stealthily approached the camp of two outlaws in the rugged Caribou country, he was, without warning, shot in the chest.

"Oh, you beggar!"

HARRY WESTAWAY, Canadian Mountie
[Union Bay, British Columbia, March 4, 1913]

Shot inside a dark general store while capturing Henry "The Flying Dutchman" Wagner, his last words were to his partner, Gordon Ross.

"Goodbye, Gordon, I'm gone."

NEPHI JENSEN, Deputy
[Near Lehi, Utah, November 22, 1913]

While tracking a murderer, he and three other lawmen were ambushed, two killed outright and Jensen dying in a rancher's cabin before a doctor could arrive.

"I don't care for myself, but I wish I could live for my wife and children."

WILLIAM TILGHMAN, Lawman
[Cromwell, Oklahoma, November 1, 1924]

Former buffalo hunter and Dodge City lawman, Tilghman, best known for his single-handed arrest of Bill Doolin, came out of retirement at the age of seventy to police the wild oil boom town of Cromwell, where he was shot, perhaps intentionally assassinated, by drunk Prohibition agent Wiley Lynn.

"Hugh, get his gun!"

GRAHAM LAMB, Sheriff
[Near Winnemucca, Nevada, October 7, 1933]

Shot trying to protect Cammie Hibbs from her former husband, he was accompanied to the hospital by Bertha Pinson Wilkerson.

I am dying . . . I don't know of anybody I would rather die for.

AND THE LAW WON

DAN HARRINGTON, Bootlegger
[Hawk Lake, Ontario, Canada, summer 1880]

Resisting arrest for bootlegging whiskey to railroad workers, Harrington raised two revolvers but was shot above the heart by Constable Ross, whose partner discouraged Ross from firing a second shot by stating that the first bullet had taken effect.

*"You're damned right it has taken effect,
but I'd sooner be shot than fined."*

HARRY BROWN, Express Company Agent
[Albuquerque, New Mexico, March 27, 1881]

He confronted Constable Milt Yarberry, his rival for a young divorcee. Yarberry settled the rivalry with several well-placed bullets.

*"Milt, I want to talk to you ... I want you to understand I
am not afraid of you and would not be even if you were marshal of the United States."*

W. P. PATTERSON, Cattleman
[Colorado City, Texas, May 16, 1881]

He fired at and was gunned down by three Texas Rangers, who accused him of firing his gun in town and wanted to examine it.

"Damn you, you will have to go examine somebody else's pistol!"

JOHN J. MCGINNIS, Outlaw
[Near Cheyenne, Wyoming, February 19, 1880]

As a prisoner of Sheriff Morrison, who was taking him to jail in Cheyenne, he separated himself from the others in the escort and made a futile break for freedom.

*"I'd just as soon take my chances with you here as
to go down to be hung by that mob."*

JIM WEBB, Fugitive
[Woodford, Oklahoma, June 15, 1884]

Wanted for murder, he was shot resisting arrest by Deputy U.S. Marshal Bass Reeves, who talked to him until he died.

*"Give me your hand, Bass. You are a brave, brave man. I
want you to accept my revolver and scabbard as a present,
and you must accept them. Take it, for with it I have killed
eleven men, four of them in the Indian Territory, and I ex-
pected you to make the twelfth."*

ANDY BLEVINS, Horse Thief
[Holbrook, Arizona, September 4, 1887]

Standing in the doorway of his house, he refused to be arrested and was shot by famous sheriff Commodore Perry Owens.

"Oh Commodore, don't do that!"

LEE RENFRO, Outlaw
[White Mountains, Arizona, September 1887]

Tracked down by lawmen who wanted to question him about a murder, Renfro, friend of Ike Clanton, resisted arrest and was shot, dying within minutes.

"Did you shoot me for money?"

WILLIAM TOWERLY, Outlaw
[Near Atoka, Indian Territory, December 1887]

Trapped by lawmen Ed Stokley and Bill Moody, he emptied his revolver, killing Stokley. He threw the empty weapon to his father before Moody killed him.

"Reload it and throw it back so I can kill that other damned marshal!"

SANTIAGO SOTIAS, Murder Suspect
[Tecate, California-Mexico border, April 1896]

Though unarmed, he appeared to reach for a weapon when Deputy Thing said, "Santiago, I want you."

"Well, you'll never get me."

BILL "KID" JOHNSON, Outlaw
[Near Fort Apache, Arizona, July 30 1898]

Wounded in a shootout with lawmen, he suffered for a day before death relieved him.

"Tell Father not to grieve after me. I brought it all on myself. Tell him to hold no one responsible for my death. Just tell him, boys, that Bill said, 'Goodbye.' "

J. C. BROWN, Horse Thief
[Bonnabel's Place, Montana, April 29, 1908]

At an isolated ranch, Brown, known as the "Pigeon-Toed Kid," resisted arrest—one shot in the solar plexus and his ridin' and writin' days were over.

"Get me a piece of paper ... I'm dying."

LOUIS KAMERAD, Fugitive
[Near Arcadia, Nebraska, April 5, 1917]

Having escaped from jail, Kamerad, the murderer of a little girl, was spotted hiding on the rafters of a barn. With the posse's guns pointing up at him, he was told to descend.

"I won't come down. You'd better shoot."

147

THE LINCOLN COUNTY WAR

The residents of Lincoln County, New Mexico, a vast county remote from the law and order of Santa Fe, had a tendency to solve their problems with guns. Through the 1870s and the early 1880s, the racial animosity between the Spanish-speaking natives and the white Americans, the opportunities for financial exploitation, and the rugged freedom of a predominantly male population made Lincoln County a hotbed of violence. When Englishman John Tunstall attempted to break the financial monopoly held by the Murphy-Dolan enterprise, he sparked a series of events that has become known as the Lincoln County War. The war and its aftermath claimed the lives of many, including its most notable warrior, William H. Bonney, Billy the Kid.

FRANK P. CAHILL
[Camp Grant, New Mexico, August 18, 1877]

He gave a statement the day after provoking and being shot by eighteen-year-old Henry Antrim, who later changed his name to William H. Bonney. Cahill, therefore, has the distinction of being the first man killed by Billy the Kid.

"I, Frank P. Cahill, being convinced that I am about to die, do make the following as my final statement: My name is Frank P. Cahill. I was born in the county and town of Galway, Ireland: yesterday, Aug. 17th, 1877, I had some trouble with Henry Antrem, otherwise known as Kid, dur-

ing which he shot me. I had called him a pimp, and he called me a son of a bitch, we then took hold of each other: I did not hit him, I think: saw him go for his pistol, and tried to get ahold of it, but could not and he shot me in the belly. I have a sister named Margaret Flannigan living at East Cambridge, Mass. And another named Kate Conden, living in San Francisco."

JOHN HENRY TUNSTALL, Rancher
[Lincoln County, New Mexico, February 18, 1878]

On his way into the town of Lincoln, he was separated from his ranch employees, among whom were Billy the Kid and John Middleton who, from a distance, shouted a warning that a hostile posse was approaching.

"What, John? What, John?"

BILLY MORTON, Gunman
[Near Lincoln, New Mexico, March 9, 1878]

Captured by a quasi-legal posse consisting of men who had once worked for John Tunstall, Morton and two others who had been involved in the Tunstall murder were killed as they were being escorted back to Lincoln. The evening before Morton's death, the group stopped for the night and allowed him to write a letter.

"The Constable himself said he was sorry we gave up as he had not wished to take us alive. We arrived here last night en route for Lincoln. I have heard that we are not to be taken alive to that place ... I am not at all afraid of their killing me, but if they should do so I wish the matter should be investigated."

FRANK BAKER, Gunman
[Near Lincoln, New Mexico, March 9, 1878]

Captured along with Billy Morton and William McCloskey, Baker spoke to young Sallie Chisum before the posse left the ranch, taking Baker to his doom. He, Morton, and McCloskey were murdered by the posse on the way to Lincoln.

"I want to make my last request on earth to you, Miss Chisum. I will never live to get to Lincoln. When you hear of my death, I wish you would send my watch and bridle, which I plaited myself, to my sweetheart and mail this letter to her."

GEORGE HINDMAN, Deputy
[Lincoln, New Mexico, April 1, 1878]

As Hindman, Sheriff Brady, and two others walked down Lincoln's main street to the courthouse, they were ambushed by Billy the Kid and five other Regulators, Brady being killed instantly and Hindman dying slowly in the street as the gunfight continued.

"Water ..."

ANDREW L. "BUCKSHOT" ROBERTS
[Blazer's Mill, New Mexico, April 5, 1878]

Another victim of the Lincoln County War, he was caught by fourteen of his enemies, including Billy the Kid, but fought it out, killing Dick Brewer, the leader of the Regulators, and receiving a mortal wound with which Dr. Blazer offered to help.

"I'm killed. No one can help me. It's all over."

FRANK MCNAB

[Near Lincoln, New Mexico, April 29, 1878]

Before being shot down by enemies, McNab, new leader of the Regulators after the death of Dick Brewer at Blazer's Mill, yelled a warning to his companion.

"For Christ's sake, let that horse go and get to cover! They'll cut you to pieces out there!"

ALEXANDER A. MCSWEEN, Lawyer

[Lincoln, New Mexico, July 19, 1878]

In the climax of the Lincoln County War, McSween, former lawyer and partner of John Tunstall, was trapped in his home with Billy the Kid and several others. While most of them escaped, McSween told the posse who surrounded his burning home that he would surrender, stepped out unarmed, made his final statement, and died in a blast of gunfire.

"I shall never surrender!"

HUSTON CHAPMAN, Lawyer

[Lincoln, New Mexico, February 18, 1879]

Surrounded and taunted by Lincoln County War gunmen who wanted to "make him dance," he refused and was shot by Billy Campbell, whose gun went off in reaction to another shot.

"My God, I am killed!"

JOHN JONES, Cowboy
[Lincoln County, New Mexico, September 1879]

Gun in hand, he confronted lawman Bob Olinger, who replied to Jones' bullet with three of his own.

"I came to settle with you about those lies I've heard you told about my killing John Beckwith."

TOM O'FOLLIARD, Outlaw
[Fort Sumner, New Mexico, December 19, 1880]

Before asking for his last drink of water, O'Folliard, shot by Pat Garrett's posse in their hunt for Billy the Kid and his companions, cursed Garrett, who reminded O'Folliard that he shouldn't curse with death only minutes away.

"Aw, go to hell, you long-legged son of a bitch."

CHARLIE BOWDRE, Outlaw
[Stinking Springs, New Mexico, December 23, 1880]

Mortally wounded by Pat Garrett, Bowdre was encouraged by the trapped Billy the Kid to leave their hideout and, gun in hand, advance on Garrett and his posse.

"I wish ... I wish ... I wish ... I'm dying."

ROBERT OLINGER, Deputy
[Lincoln, New Mexico, April 28, 1881]

Moments after being told that his prisoner, Billy the Kid, had killed his other guard, he looked up to a second-story window to see the Kid pointing Olinger's own shotgun at him.

"Yes, and he's killed me too."

"BILLY THE KID," HENRY ANTRIM
Alias William Bonney, Outlaw
[Fort Sumner, New Mexico, July 14, 1881]

Late at night, startled by coming upon two men on the steps of Pete Maxwell's veranda, he moved through the open doorway of Maxwell's bedroom, not realizing that the shadowy figure sitting beside Maxwell's bed was Sheriff Pat Garrett.

"Quienes son esos hombres afuera, Pete?"
[Who are those fellows outside, Pete?]

[Sees Garrett] *"Quien es? Quien es?"* [Who is it?]

BAD JUDGMENT

S. H. JACKSON, Bartender
[Raton, New Mexico, June 26, 1882]

Being a good citizen, he joined in the chase for fugitive Gus Mentzer and spotted him as Mentzer ran in front of a locomotive's headlight, Jackson's alarm prompting Mentzer to stop long enough to shoot.

"There he is !"

HARVEY MOULTON, Justice of the Peace
[Raton, New Mexico, June 26, 1882]

After fugitive Gus Mentzer, who had killed two pursuers, S. H. Jackson and Moulton's partner Hugh Eddleson, was finally captured, Moulton demanded that the deputy sheriff give over the prisoner for immediate trial and, when the deputy refused, attacked the deputy, both men dying in the gunfight.

"If the town is to be run by a gambler I would rather die or leave. Give up the son of a bitch to be hung!"

WILLIAM RADER, Deputy
[Near Castle, Montana, April, 1893]

In the attempt to arrest Bill Gay and Gay's brother-in-law, he shot at Gay and saw him fall from what turned out to be a leg wound, then unwisely left his partner and approached the fallen Gay.

"You hold the horses; I think I have broken that fellow's back."

DUDLEY CHAMPION, Cowboy
[Near Lusk, Wyoming, May, 1893]

Confronted by Mike Shonsey, stock detective, who had feuded with Dudley's brother, Nate, during the Johnson County War, he lost his battle because of a defective gun.

"I can't cock it! I can't cock it!"

SAM FARRIS, Deputy
[Yukon, Oklahoma Territory, May 21, 1894]

Underestimating the seriousness of the situation, he attempted to arrest two fugitives who immediately shot him.

"I have a telegram requesting the arrest of you men. Come in here and I will read it to you."

ANDREW BALFOUR, Sheriff
[Pryor's Grove, Kansas, July 4, 1894]

He finally caught up to Zip Wyatt, who immediately shot him.

"Zip, I've got a warrant for you."

COLIN CAMPBELL COLEBROOK, Sergeant,
North-West Mounted Police
[Near Kinistino, Northwest Territories, Canada, October 29, 1895]

Attempting to arrest Almighty Voice for cattle theft, he kept approaching though the Indian covered him with his rifle and warned him away.

"Come on, old boy ... come on, old boy."

VALENTINE S. HOY, Rancher
[Near Vermillion Creek, Colorado, March 1, 1898]

Part of a posse searching for the killer of fifteen-year-old Willie Strang, he bravely approached Dave Lant and dangerous Harry Tracy, who wasn't convinced.

"We don't want you, Tracy. It's Johnson we want ...
this is not your fight."

M. E. CONRAD, Deputy/Detective
[Kokomo, Colorado, August 12, 1898]

Barging into the cabin of four suspected robbers who had guns hidden in their beds, he refused to buy their story and learned the truth the hard way.

"Boys, we must see what you have got under those blankets."

WARREN BAXTER EARP, Cattle Detective
[Willcox, Arizona, July 6, 1900]

Trusting to the old code, the youngest of the famous Earp brothers kept advancing, holding his coat open, even though his enemy had fired at him and was still pointing his gun.

"I have not got any arm. You have a good deal the best of this."

JACK SULLY, Rustler
[Near Lucas, South Dakota, May 17(?), 1904]

Cornered by lawmen, he refused to surrender, mounted, and attempted to outrun them.

"Goodbye to all. With fair play I equal three of them."

MIKE RYAN, Con Man
[Sheridan, Colorado, July 5, 1904]

Belligerently insulting a woman in the company of Sheriff Hoolahan, who threatened to arrest him, he made the final mistake of going for his gun and grabbing the right hand of the left-handed sheriff.

"I'll get you right now, damn you!"

W. W. GREER, Duck Raiser
[Near Culbertson, Montana, February 1, 1905]

A loner, the antisocial "Duck Man," accusing an innocent young visitor of being a horse thief, raised his shotgun but was killed by two bullets, his last words inserted between the two shots.

"I'll get you yet."

DAVE "BUD" BALLEW, Former Deputy Sheriff
[Wichita Falls, Texas, May 5, 1922]

Drunk and in a mood to celebrate with his six-gun, the killer of Dow Braziel and twelve other men refused to be arrested and drew when the City Marshal asked for his guns.

"You are out of luck!"

157

EL PASO

JOHN HALE, Rancher
[El Paso, Texas, April 14, 1881]

Drunk, he fired the first shot in El Paso's famous gunbattle, killing Gus Krempkau, who managed to kill Hale in return.

"Turn loose, Campbell! I've got him covered!"

DALLAS STOUDENMIRE, El Paso Marshal
[El Paso, Texas, September 18, 1882]

Dr. Manning's accusation that Stoudenmire did not stick to a previous agreement led to a violent confrontation.

"Whoever says I have not tells a damn lie!"

JOE MCKIDRICT, Texas Ranger
[El Paso, Texas, April 3, 1894]

Hearing gunfire at Tillie Howard's whorehouse, he came running and questioned drunk Bass Outlaw, who put a bullet in McKidrict's head.

"Bass, why did you shoot?"

BAZ LAMAR "BASS" OUTLAW, Former Texas Ranger
[El Paso, Texas, April 3, 1894]

Shot by Constable John Selman immediately after the McKidrict killing, Outlaw was taken into the back room of a saloon, where he struggled with death.

"Oh, God, help! Where are my friends?"

MARTIN M'ROSE, Fugitive
[El Paso, Texas, June 29, 1895]

Enticed by lawman George Scarborough to cross the bridge from Juarez to El Paso, he was ambushed by Scarborough's companions, Jeff Milton and Frank McMahon.

"Boys, you've killed me. Don't shoot anymore."

JOHN WESLEY HARDIN, Lawyer/Ex-Gunfighter
[El Paso, Texas, August 19, 1895]

While rolling dice for drinks in the Acme Saloon, Hardin, who had the reputation of being the West's most deadly gunman, was shot in the back of the head by Constable John Selman.

"Brown, you've got four sixes to beat."

JOHN SELMAN, Constable
[El Paso, Texas, April 6, 1896]

The infamous killer of John Wesley Hardin, Selman, gunned down in an alley by renowned lawman George Scarborough, lived for a day, dying after an operation.

"George Scarborough came downstairs and we spoke friendly together. He put his arm around my neck and said 'Uncle John, I want to see you', and he led me out to the alley and before I knew he had shot me in the neck and I fell. I said, 'My God, George, do you intend to kill me this way?' I reached for my pistol but didn't have it ..."

[Later] *"Boys, you know I am not afraid of any man, but I never drew my gun."*

GERONIMO PARRA, Outlaw
[El Paso, Texas, January 6, 1900]

Guilty of killing a Ranger, he stabbed the two guards who came to escort him to the gallows from which he soon swung.

[In Spanish] *"Gentlemen, I bid you all farewell, and of those whom I have offended in the last few minutes I ask pardon. I am going to die unjustly."*

MANEN CLEMENTS, Former Constable
[El Paso, Texas, December 29, 1908]

Following a heated dispute in the Coney Island Saloon, he was shot in the back of the head by an unknown assassin.

"If anybody says that I offered to do that for one thousand dollars they are a damned liar!"

TOMBSTONE, ARIZONA

MIKE D. KILLEEN
[Tombstone, Arizona, June 27, 1880]

Mortally wounded in a gunfight, he lingered for five days and gave a dying statement. After his death, his wife married Frank Leslie.

"At the ball I wanted to see my wife. I heard that she had gone home with Leslie, and when I was told she had gone home I went down to the hotel with the expectation of finding both of them in Leslie's room, but they were not there; meanwhile, I started towards the porch, having heard voices, and I thought it might be them; I got to the door of the porch and satisfied myself she and Leslie were sitting side by side, his arm around her waist; that settled it; I thought I would go off now; started back again; Perine came along pistol in hand and knowing him to be a particular friend of Leslie I looked for trouble as in the early part of the evening he went into Tasker & Hoke's and bought a box of cartridges and filled all chambers of his pistol and deposited the remainder of the box with me; I started away from the porch when Perine came along and yelled out, "Look out Frank, there is Mike." With that Leslie rose from his chair in a half standing position, pulling his pistol; he fired the pistol at me and

I fired one shot at him; I saw I was in for it and I made a jump and caught the pistol and beat him over the head with mine, which I had in my hand at the time; I happened to look and saw Perine standing in the door with his pistol leveled at me; he pulled the trigger, which he repeated twice, firing in all three shots; by this time I had used up Leslie pretty well; then turned and jumped and caught Perine's pistol, and did the same to him; by this time people commenced to congregate and I dropped this man, not thinking of my own wounds; all I knew was I was shot in the nose somewhere. I fired two shots myself intentionally, and every time I would strike the pistol went off accidentally; fired at Perine when he fired at me; one shot was at Perine and one at Leslie; fired at Leslie when he pulled his revolver first and stood in a half stooping position; this was right after he first fired at me."

THOMAS HARPER, Cowboy
[Tombstone, Arizona, July 8, 1881]

Convicted of murdering an unarmed man, Harper wrote a final message to his friend, Curley Bill Brocious:

"Curley, you are aware that I am not in the habit of lecturing any man, but in this case you may remember the words of a dying man (for I am all to intents and purposes such), and perhaps give heed to them. . . . Curley, I want you to take warning by me. Do not be too handy with a pistol. Keep cool and never fire at a man unless in the actual defense of your life. You must stand a heap from a man before you kill him. Words do not hurt, so you must never mind what is said to aggravate you. As I said before, don't try and hunt a row. Give my kind regards to any of my old friends who you may chance to meet, and tell them to take a warning by me. I bear no ill will, and I think I am going to die in peace. Hoping you will take heed of what I write, I am, as ever, your unfortunate friend. THOMAS HARPER."

TOM McLAURY, Cowboy
[Tombstone, Arizona, October 26, 1881]

He opened his coat moments before being blasted with a shotgun in the hands of Doc Holliday during the gunfight at the OK Corral.

"I'm not armed!"

BILLY CLANTON, Cowboy
[Tombstone, Arizona, October 26, 1881]

Though shot several times by the Earps and Doc Holliday in the famous gunfight at the OK Corral, he lingered for several hours before dying.

"Get a doctor and put me to sleep ... Pull off my boots. I always told my mother I'd never die with my boots on ..."

[Later] *"They've murdered me! Clear the crowd away from the door and give me air. I've been murdered ..."*

[Later] *"Drive the crowd away."*

ZWING HUNT, Outlaw
[Russel's Canyon, Arizona, May 31, 1882]

After being seriously wounded by officers and held in the Tombstone hospital, Hunt, despite his wound, escaped with the help of his brother and hid in the Chiricahua mountains, only to be discovered and attacked a month later by Indians.

"Damn it! Go to shooting!"

MORGAN EARP
[Tombstone, Arizona, March 18, 1882]

In retaliation for his part in the gunfight at the OK Corral, while playing pool he was shot from behind, the bullet hitting his spine, making it impossible for him to stand up. He whispered to his brother Wyatt and, though no one but Wyatt heard him, one source claims that Morgan asked Wyatt,

"Do you know who did it?"

When Wyatt promised to get revenge, Morgan supposedly said,

"That's all I ask. But Wyatt, be careful."

As he was carried to the pool table, Morgan said in pain,

"Don't, boys, don't. I can't stand it.
I have played my last game of pool."

FRANK STILWELL, Cowboy
[Tucson, Arizona, March 20, 1882]

After being part of the gang that gunned down Morgan Earp, Stilwell and others tried to ambush Virgil and Wyatt Earp at the Tucson train station. In the dark, Wyatt spotted the assassins and went out to challenge them. Stilwell advanced without drawing his pistol but attempted to grab Earp's shotgun, inexplicably uttering the name of Earp's dead brother just before Earp blasted the confused Stilwell with both barrels.

"Morg! Morg!"

GEORGE JOHNSON, Stagecoach Robber
[Tombstone, Arizona, October 1882]

The news that his victim had died, not of a gunshot, but of a heart attack, came too late to save him from a lynch mob.

"I have had my share of life. I chose to live on the wrong side of the law, but I do not regret it. I am sorry for those I have shot, and I imagine I shall be meeting some of them soon. I request a Christian burial."

THOMAS HALDERMAN, Rustler/Murderer
[Tombstone, Arizona, November 16, 1900]

On the gallows, he and his twenty-three-year-old brother, William, put on a show of bravado.

"Hello, hombres. The sun's hot, ain't it? . . . Those people look all right . . . I have nothing to say and guess it would not do any good anyway. I forgive you all and hope you will forgive me . . . Goodbye, boys. Pray for us. Goodbye."

WILLIAM HALDERMAN, Rustler/Murderer
[Tombstone, Arizona, November 16, 1900]

On the gallows, with his twenty-year-old brother, Thomas.

"Nice looking crowd . . . Some of you fellers are shaking already . . . This will be an experience that ought to benefit all of you. I hope I will meet you all. I pray for you and hope you will pray for me . . . Goodbye, boys. Pray for us. Goodbye.

FUN AND GAMES

HENRY KAPANICK, Deputy
[Faribault, Minnesota, October 2, 1876]

Having made a five-dollar bet that he could get inside the heavily guarded jail where the Younger brothers were incarcerated after the Northfield bank robbery attempt, Kapanick took the forthright approach, merely trying to walk past the night guard, who asked for identification and then fired when Kapanick did not stop.

"Don't you know I'm a policeman?"

JOHN JOHNSON, Miner
[Alma, Colorado, January 25, 1880]

After cards and drinks and the fun of knocking each other's hat off, he found that his friend Simms, who had suddenly lost his sense of humor, was ordering him, at gunpoint, to pick up the hat.

"I won't do it."

M. S. McCray
[Deming, New Mexico, August 21, 1881]

Interrupted in his restaurant meal by boisterous, dish-breaking "Frank Over the Fence," he scolded the drunk badman, who stuck his six-shooter in McCray's face.

"You wouldn't shoot me for that, would you?"

I. T. McCray, Cowboy
[White Oaks, New Mexico, May 31, 1880]

Having issued a challenge to fight, he saw his opponent, who thought a fistfight was meant, begin to unbuckle his gunbelt.

"I will shoot you—twenty steps!"

James H. Williams, Texas Ranger
[Big Springs, Texas, September 15, 1881]

While he was inquiring for lodgings for the night, an acquaintance inexplicably began shooting, presumably not with the intention of hitting anyone.

"I'm struck. The third shot got me ... Telegraph McMurry at Colorado City ... It was an accident."

Lewis "Juaquin" Adams
[Casper, Wyoming, April 12, 1892]

During an argument in a poker game, he picked up a pool cue and advanced upon Jeff Dunbar, who was holding a better hand—a revolver.

"Shoot away! It's fine music to my ears!"

WILLIAM SHURBURT, Cement Mason
[Phoenix, Arizona, October 9, 1894]

The day after catching William Price cheating in a poker game, he, unarmed, was shot four times by Price and lingered in agony for twenty-six hours with his wife beside him.

"Goodbye, I'm going now."

JEFF DUNBAR, Outlaw
[Dixon, Wyoming, July 24, 1898]

Cashing in his chips with the bartender, before going for his gun he first made reference to an old gambling debt owed to him by the bartender, who was accurate enough to cancel the debt.

"You tried to run it over me last winter, didn't you? You can't run nothing over me!"

DANGEROUS OCCUPATIONS

FADDIMAN, Bartender
[Pioche, Nevada, c. 1870]

He spoke his last words to a hostile drunk.

"You don't need another drink."

R. A. C. MARTIN, Bank Cashier
[Columbia, Kentucky, April 29, 1872]

He uttered the warning that prompted the Jesse James gang to shoot him dead.

"Bank robbers!"

MARY GIBSON, Saloon Owner
[Sacramento, California, September 1872]

When she caught her "guests" trying to rob her, she was beaten by Charles Mortimer, whose partner, Carrie Spencer, then cut Gibson's throat.

"The damned bitch had her hand in my pocket."

DAVE MULLEN, Dance House Owner
[Bismarck, Dakota Territory, November 11, 1873]

Having given sanctuary to a friend who had killed a soldier the day before, Mullen was aroused from his sleep by a large group of soldiers demanding entrance and seeking revenge. With his bartender, Dennis Hennefin, an unarmed Mullen unwisely opened the door.

"Hold on, boys. I'll let you in. "

[Soldier: "No shooting, Dave."] *"All right. I have nothing on me."*

[Opens door, shots] *"Oh! Denny! Denny! Denny!"*

L. B. HASBROUCK, Lawyer
[Caldwell, Kansas, July 29, 1874]

Implicated in a complex plot of theft and murder, he and two suspected cohorts were taken from the jail and lynched. His last concerns were that a fifteen-dollar debt be paid and that his parents not be informed of the lynching.

"Sell my saddle and bridle and pay him . . . I would not have them know this for the world."

JACK O'NEIL, Dance House Owner
[Bismarck, Dakota Territory, December 12, 1874]

Having earlier argued with, and threatened to kill, gambler Paddy Hall, O'Neil left a saloon and walked into the gun of his enemy.

"I am going home, and will be sober in the morning."

MOLLY BRENNAN, Dance Hall Girl
[Sweetwater, Texas, January 24, 1876]

In the Lady Gay dance hall, to protect her new beau, Bat Masterson, she jumped in front of him, taking the bullet from her former boyfriend, Sergeant Melvin King, who became Masterson's first, and possibly only, victim.

"Don't shoot! You're drunk!"

CHARLES NOLIN, Mail Carrier
[Near Sturgis, Dakota Territory, August 19, 1876]

Before continuing his Sidney-Deadwood mail run, he ate supper with some freighters who tried to convince him to stay the night and avoid the Sioux who, bold and troublesome after their victory at the Little Bighorn, finally got him.

"The boys in Deadwood are waiting for news from their homes. The mail must go through."

MARK WILSON, Theater Owner
[Austin, Texas, December 25, 1876]

Moments before being shot and killed by renowned gunman Ben Thompson, he pointed a shotgun at Thompson in his crowded bar.

"Clear the way there!"

ANNIE FERGUSON, Prostitute
[Cheyenne, Wyoming, April 1877]

After a severe beating by another prostitute, Annie was put to bed but died during the night.

"Fanny Brown gave me the beating. I am hurt inside and think I will die soon."

ALEX COOPER, Miner
[Near Bannack, Montana, August 12, 1877]

Hiding in the bushes from Nez Perce Indians, he alone of the five miners finally gave in to the promise of safety from the Indians, who then shot him with his own gun.

"Well, boys, I think I will do as they say. I am going out and give myself up."

DAN COOMBS, Freighter
[Eastern Idaho, August 15, 1877]

Captured with his companions by Nez Perce Indians who became drunk after plundering the freighters' wagons, Coombs, tormented by Indian women who poked him with firebrands, put his last words into action and precipitated the melee in which he was killed.

"The next squaw that pokes me is going to get this bullwhip over her ears!"

ANONYMOUS SOLDIER'S WIFE, Laundress
[Fort C. F. Smith, Montana, 1878]

Antagonizing her corporal husband by continual nagging, she was shot by him "in a fit of passion," though with her final breath she had the last word.

"Murderer…murderer!"

BENJAMIN C. PORTER, Actor
[Marshall, Texas, March 20, 1879]

On tour with Maurice Barrymore, father of the famous Barrymore actors, Porter attempted to protect an actress from the attentions of a gunman and was shot. Barrymore was wounded.

"Oh, my Lord, why did that man want to kill me?
What harm did I do him?"

WILLIAM CUMMINGS, Banker
[Near Nevada City, California, September 1, 1879]

During a stagecoach robbery, he was shot and killed because he refused to give up his valise, which contained $6,700 in gold bullion.

"That's my property. It's all I have in the world and
I'm going to protect it!"

DICK ELGIN, Ranch Bookkeeper
[Fort Fetterman, Wyoming, October 1882]

In a saloon, he was relaxing before being shot by frustrated cowboy Red Capp, who had just drunk up his pay and wanted some more money.

"Red, you haven't any more coming.
You are drunk and will just get into trouble."

GEORGE WOODS, Saloon/Whorehouse Proprietor
[Caldwell, Kansas, August 18, 1881]

Shot by Charlie Davis, a quarrelsome customer, his last words were to his wife, the notorious Mag Woods.

"Catch Charlie Davis and prosecute him to the full extent of the law . . . keep all the property . . . do the best you can, and be a good girl."

TOM CAIN, Dance Hall/Bordello Owner
[Ashfork, Arizona, November 27, 1884]

In an argument over eighty cents, he challenged a teamster named Evans, who protested that he was unarmed.

"Well, go and fix yourself, and that God damn quick, too, and I'll settle this matter with you."

[Evans, returned, with shotgun: "Are you ready?"] *"Yes!"*

NELSON W. STARBIRD, Hack Driver
[West Las Vegas, New Mexico, April 8, 1880]

Driving passengers home, one of whom might have been carrying a large sum of money, he was shot as he tried to bypass three men who wanted the carriage to stop.

*"Oh, my God, I'm shot in the arm . . .
take the reins . . . I'm fainting."*

GEORGE DOUGLAS WYATT, School Division Secretary
[Near Jefferson, Park County, Colorado, May 6, 1895]

Mortally wounded at a school board meeting in the schoolhouse by an angry citizen, he lingered long enough to dictate a statement.

"I, George Douglas Wyatt, realizing my condition to be precarious, do depose and say: I was shot by Benjamin Radcliff, as was also Samuel Taylor and Lincoln F. McCurdy. Taylor was shot first, McCurdy next, then myself. No one else was armed: no blows were struck before the shooting. A heated discussion preceded the shooting. Radcliff claimed that we (Taylor, McCurdy, and myself) had slandered him and said he had an intrigue with his own daughter. No attempt was made by any of the parties to assault Radcliff. Five shots were fired. The first shot was accidental and struck the floor in front of Taylor. A few minutes elapsed between the first and second shots. The second shot struck Taylor. Two shots were fired at McCurdy and one shot was fired at myself. I was shot at the far end of the room, looking from the door. Radcliff stood near the door, behind the seats, when he fired the shots. No conversation took place after the first shot was fired."

LAWRENCE KEATING, Prison Guard
[United States Jail, Fort Smith, Arkansas, July 26, 1895]

Shot by Cherokee Bill during an attempted jailbreak, he spoke his last words to fellow guard Will Lawson.

"Kill the dog, Will; he has killed me."

ED JENNINGS, Lawyer
[Woodward, Oklahoma, October 8, 1895]

After angrily battling fellow lawyer Temple Houston in court that day, he continued the fight in the evening when Houston wanted to see him outside the saloon.

"See me here and now, you son of a bitch!"

DANIEL CUMMINGS, Sheepherder
[Near Brown Ranch, Idaho, February 4, 1896]

Shot by a cattleman and left to die at his sheep camp, he managed to leave a note.

"If I die, bury me. Take care of my sisters."

FRANK CARPENTER, Miner
[Turret, Colorado, August 25, 1902]

When the hoisting equipment failed, stalling the ore bucket in which he and his partner were being raised out of the shaft where seven dynamite charges were fizzing, Carpenter panicked, trying repeatedly to climb the greasy cable until he fell down the shaft where he was blown to pieces a minute after the bucket was successfully raised to the surface.

"Oh, my God!"

WILLIAM CHOUNARD, Whorehouse Piano Player
[Walker, Minnesota, August 30, 1904]

He killed a whore named Dora, doubting her faithfulness to him, and was hanged.

"Forgive us our trespasses And forgive those who trespass against us ..."

Sarah J. "Sally" Rooke, Telephone Operator
[Folsom, New Mexico, August 27, 1908]

As floodwaters rushed toward the town of Folsom, she stayed at her switchboard, ringing up homes and warning the residents until her home was swept away.

"Pack up and leave at once. A flood is coming down the valley!"

Anonymous Train Engineer
[Coos County, Oregon, November 25, 1912]

As the train began crossing a wooden trestle bridge over a canyon, the structure began to sway and then collapsed. As the train fell to the bottom of the canyon, killing all but one of the seven men aboard, the engineer just had time to shout out the obvious.

"Boys, we're gone!"

Wong Bock Sing, Launderer
[Boise, Idaho, March 31, 1917]

Marked as a target in a tong war, he didn't realize that the Oriental stranger who asked if there might be fan-tan gambling or opium in the back room was really a hit man from a rival tong.

"Get out! Go away! No fan-tan, no pipe! Laundry.
You go. I call police!"

177

OLA MAY POWER, Homemaker
[Aravaipa Canyon, Arizona, December 6, 1917]

Fulfilling the role of cook for her gold-mining brothers and father, she probably died of botulism, her last word arousing suspicion of murder though the inquest listed the cause of her death as "unknown."

"Poison ..."

T. J. "JEFF" POWER, Goldminer
[Aravaipa Canyon, Arizona, February 10, 1918]

Hearing noises outside the cabin in which he and his suspicious sons lived, he came to the door and put down his rifle at the request of law officers who then shot him and who were in turn killed by his sons.

"Why did Kane Wootan shoot me when I had my hands up?"

COYL JOHNSON, Brakeman
[Near Siskiyou Station, Oregon, October 11, 1923]

In the West's last great train robbery, he was told by one of the DeAutremont brothers to go forward with instructions, but, as he emerged from the smoke of the dynamite blast, the other two brothers, in a panic, shot him down.

"Wait a minute, boys! That other fella back there said to pull ahead."

POLITICS

JOSEPH SMITH, Mormon Leader
[Carthage, Illinois, June 27, 1844]

Fighting anti-Mormon sentiment, Smith, the founder of the Mormon Church, was charged with treason and held in jail until a mob broke in and shot him and his brother.

[Letter to his wife, Emma, written in jail] *"I am very much resigned to my lot, knowing I am justified, and have done the best that could be done. Give my love to the children and all my friends ... May God bless you all."*

[Seeing his brother shot] *"Oh dear brother Hyrum!"*

[Shot four times, Joseph fell out the window] *"Oh Lord! My God!"*

HYRUM SMITH, Mormon Leader
[Carthage, Illinois, June 27, 1844]

Held in jail with his brother Joseph, he was shot by the mob made up of local militia.

"I am a dead man!"

JAMES P. CASEY, Politician
[San Francisco, California, May 22, 1856]

A crooked politician and a bully, he lost courage when he was lynched before seven thousand spectators for killing an editor.

"Mercy ... poor mother ..."

WESLEY COATES, Republican
[Little Lake, California, October 16, 1867]

When the Coates and Frost families brought their political feud to town on election day, a wild shootout erupted after a Frost in-law stated he could whip any Republican in town.

"I am your man. Just walk out and try it. .... You can't do it!"

E. P. WEBER, County Commissioner
[Grand Lake, Colorado, July 4, 1883]

He and two other commissioners were attacked by masked political opponents near their hotel on their way to attend to official business.

"I hope there won't be any more killing."

CHARLES W. ROYER, Sheriff
[Georgetown, Colorado, July 16, 1883]

In fear of being discovered as one of the masked men who attacked the three commissioners at Grand Lake, he confessed to a friend, then went to his room and shot himself.

"Day dodged back behind the ice-house, and as he came around the south side of it he met Bill Redman. He shot at Redman, breaking his right arm and shooting the gun out of his hand. Just then I raised up out of my hiding place and

shot Day. I shot him through the heart and his head fell back in the lake. Ever since I killed him, who I considered my best friend in the Park, old Barney has been looking me in the eye. Ad, I can't stand it any longer. I can't make a move that I am not watched, and it is only a question of time before it will come to a showdown. I have decided to make a short work of the whole mess."

WILLIAM REDMAN, Deputy
[Near Dog Creek, Utah, July 1883]

Wounded while attacking the three commissioners at Grand Lake, he disappeared into the wilderness, only to commit suicide after leaving his last words written in the sand near his body.

"I am William Redman."

REV. GEORGE CHANNING HADDOCK, Minister
[Sioux City, Iowa, August 3, 1886]

Despite a warning, and armed only with a cane and a piece of iron, the avid prohibitionist walked into the street, where he was shot by anti-prohibition thugs.

"Well, I can take care of myself and them too."

JIM GARVEY, Sheriff
[Richmond, Texas, August 16, 1889]

When feuding political factions drew guns on each other, he tried to maintain order but, despite the presence of Sergeant Ira Aten and his Texas Rangers, all hell broke loose.

"Never, Aten. I am sheriff of this county and am going to handle this situation myself. You keep out of it."

TOM PINCKNEY
[Hempstead, Texas, April 25, 1905]

He was shot twice in the back at a Prohibition League meeting at which three other men, including his brother, died.

"If I wanted to shoot a man, I wouldn't shoot him in the back."

DOW BRAZIEL, U.S. Marshal
[Ardmore, Oklahoma, January 19, 1919]

Surprised by the chief of police and a deputy sheriff with whom he had political and personal difficulties, he got the worst of the shootout even though he was considered the fastest gun of his day in southern Oklahoma.

"He pulled a gun on me—you saw him—you know he did!"

THE RIEL REBELLION

In 1885 the Metis people, who had fled from the Red River
Settlement in Manitoba fifteen years earlier, were again threatened with the loss of their lands as the Canadian surveyors
moved across the Saskatchewan prairie. The Metis elders called
for the return of their former leader Louis David Riel, exiled in
Montana. Riel returned and led a rebellion, enlisting the aid of
some Indian bands. The rebellion took the form of several skir-
mishes, battles at Duck Lake and Fish Creek, a massacre of civil-
ians at Frog Lake, and a final resounding defeat at Batoche. Riel
was captured and hanged for treason.

THOMAS SCOTT, Settler
[Fort Garry (Winnipeg), Assiniboia Territory, March 4, 1870]

Sentenced to be executed for his part in attempting to wrest Fort
Garry from the possession of Louis Riel and the Metis settlers
who had captured it to forestall the transfer of Assiniboia to
Canada, he was first hit twice by the firing squad, then shot
again in the head.

*"This is horrible! This is cold-blooded murder! Be sure to
make a true statement!"*

ISIDORE DUMONT, Metis

[Duck Lake, Northwest Territories, Canada, March 26, 1885]

When North-West Mounted Police approached Duck Lake with a view to confiscating weapons from the Indians, Metis leader Gabriel Dumont and his warriors intercepted them. Dumont sent ahead his brother, Isidore, to speak with police interpreter "Gentleman Joe" McKay, who was arguing with Assiyiwin. When the argument turned violent, Dumont shouted,

"Don't shoot each other! We want to find a way to work this out peacefully! We don't want anyone killed!"

McKay, suspecting he was being trapped, shot Dumont in the head.

ASSIYIWIN, Cree Chief

[Duck Lake, Northwest Territories, Canada, March 27, 1885]

Knowing that North-West Mounted Police were heading toward Duck Lake to confiscate weapons and that there was a possibility of violence, Assiyiwin, hurrying home, encountered police interpreter "Gentleman Joe" McKay, who was some distance ahead of the main force. When someone in the distance asked him if he understood what was happening, the poor-sighted Assiyiwin responded,

"No, I am blind. Tell me what is going on."

Told by McKay to go back, Assiyiwin replied,

"If you are going to have a battle, if you are going to spill blood, you cannot do it on our reserve land."

Again told to go back, Assiyiwan became defiant, making it clear that he intended to go forward:

"No. I am going home."

Warned not to approach, the once powerful warrior grabbed McKay's rifle and struggled with him. McKay drew a revolver, shot Isidore Dumont, and then shot Assiyiwin in the stomach.

184

Assiyiwin was later taken to Duck Lake, where he died before sunrise. His and Dumont's death set off the Battle of Duck Lake, the first violent encounter of the Riel Rebellion.

JAMES BAKELY, Civilian Volunteer
[Duck Lake, Northwest Territories, Canada, March 26, 1885]

Lacking battle experience, and perhaps caution as well, he was shot by Metis rebels who did not provide the easy fight the Canadian volunteers were expecting.

"God have mercy on my soul."

WILLIAM NAPIER, Civilian Volunteer
[Duck Lake, Northwest Territories, Canada, March 26, 1885]

Inexperienced in battle, he was one of several casualties at the Duck Lake battle against Metis fighters.

"Tell my father and mother that I died happy, fighting for my Queen and country."

THOMAS TRUEMAN QUINN, Indian Agent
[Frog Lake, Northwest Territories, Canada, April 2, 1885]

Survivor of the Minnesota Sioux Uprising, in which his father was killed, Quinn stood his ground when Big Bear's Cree warriors captured the settlement of Frog Lake. Perhaps realizing that he was doomed, he showed no fear when his killer, war chief Wandering Spirit, ordered him, at gunpoint, to accompany the war party. Quinn told the warrior,

"My place is here. Big Bear has not asked me to leave.
I will not go."

Wandering Spirit, without hesitating, killed Quinn.

JOHN WILLISCROFT
[Frog Lake, Northwest Territories, Canada, April 2, 1885]

Seeing the Indians shoot Quinn, seventy-five-year-old Williscroft ran, attempting to warn Gowanlock and the others. A bullet took off his hat; the next one hit him, and he ran screaming into the bushes, where he died.

"Oh, don't shoot! Don't shoot!"

JOHN GOWANLOCK, Millwright
[Frog Lake, Northwest Territories, Canada, April 2, 1885]

Just before being shot by Big Bear's Crees in the infamous Frog Lake Massacre, he and his wife were led out of the store, arm in arm. He was shot just after saying,

"My dear wife, be brave to the end."

JOHN DELANEY, Farm Instructor
[Frog Lake, Northwest Territories, Canada, April 2, 1885]

After the killing of Indian Agent Quinn, the massacre at Frog Lake began. Delaney, walking beside his wife, was shot immediately after Gowanlock. The wives of both men were taken prisoner and later released unharmed.

"I am shot!"

FATHER LEON ADELARD FAFARD
[Frog Lake, Northwest Territories, Canada, April 2, 1885]

Moments before receiving his own death wound, he rushed to the fallen John Gowanlock and administered last rites.

"My poor brother, I think you are safe with God."

DAVID COWAN, Northwest Mounted Police Constable
[Fort Pitt, Northwest Territories, Canada, April 14, 1885]

Returning to Fort Pitt after searching for Big Bear's Cree at Frog Lake, Cowan and two other scouts unexpectedly came upon a large band of warriors. Cowan's horse balked, possibly shot, and, as Cowan tried to run, an Indian rode by him but did not shoot. Cowan said to him,

"Don't shoot, my brother!"

Seconds later, he fell, shot through the heart by another brave.

OLD CREE WOMAN
[Near Fort Pitt, Northwest Territories, Canada, May 1, 1885]

Deluded, perhaps deranged, and probably reacting to the white captives taken at Frog Lake, she was bludgeoned, then shot shortly before sundown by her own tribe because she had become a windigo, an evil spirit.

[Translation from Cree] *"I am bound to eat a white man's flesh before the sun goes down."*

JOHN FRENCH, Captain, Canadian Army
[Batoche, Northwest Territories, Canada, May 12, 1885]

In the final attack on Riel's forces during the Riel Rebellion, John French and Tom Hourie led the assault into the village of Batoche, where a Metis enemy, hidden in a house, shot French.

"Well, Tom, I'm shot, but never mind;
we were the first that came here."

JOSEPH OUELETTE, Metis fighter
[Batoche, Northwest Territories, Canada, May 12, 1885]

Fighting with Riel's forces in the Riel Rebellion, the ninety-three-year-old Ouelette was encouraged time and again to pull back.

"Just a minute! I want to kill another Englishman!"

LOUIS DAVID RIEL, Metis Leader
[Regina, Northwest Territories, Canada, November 16, 1885]

Convicted of treason for having led a failed rebellion, as his execution drew near, he wrote a letter to his mother, made a statement to a priest about an execution he had ordered fifteen years earlier, then was taken to the scaffold.

My Dear Mother: I received your letter of blessing and yesterday, Sunday, I asked Father Andre to place it upon the altar during the celebration of mass, that its spirit might be diffused upon me. I asked him then to place his hands on my head so that I might receive it with efficacy, since I could not go to the church, and it has thus shed upon me the graces of the mass with its abundance of benefits, spiritual and temporal.

To my wife, my children, my brothers, my sister-in-law and other relatives who are all dear to me, say farewell on my behalf.

Dear mother, it is the desire of your eldest son that your prayers for me may mount to the throne of Jesus Christ, to Mary, to Joseph, my good protector, and that the mercy and abundant consolations of God may be shed upon you, upon my wife, my children and other relatives from generation to generation—the plenitude of spiritual blessing in return for those you have called down upon me; and that they may rain especially upon you, who have been for me so good a mother. May your faith, your hope, your charity and your example be as a tree laden with abundant fruit for the pre-

188

sent and for the future. May God, when your last hour sounds, be so pleased with piety that He will cause your spirit to be borne from the earth on the wings of angels.

It is now two o'clock in the morning of this day, the last I am to pass upon this earth, and Father Andre has told me to hold myself in readiness for the great event. I have listened to him and intend to do everything according to his desires and recommendations.

God is holding me in his hand to keep me in peace and quietness, as oil is held in a vial, so none can disturb. I am doing what I can to be ready. I am even calm, in accordance with the pious exhortations of the venerable Archbishop Bourget. Yesterday and today I prayed God to reassure you and to dispense to you all manner of consolation so that your heart may not be troubled by care and anxiety. I am brave. I embrace you with all affection.

I embrace you as a son respectful to his duty; you, my dear wife, as a Christian husband in accordance with the spirit of Christian marriage; I embrace your children, entrusting them to the greatness of divine mercy. And you all, brothers and sister-in-law, relatives and friends, I embrace with all the affection with which my heart is capable.

Dear Mother, I am, your son, affectionate, obedient and submissive.

Louis David Riel.

[To the priest]

"I feel, and I swear as I am about to appear before God that I speak the truth, that the shooting of Scott was not a crime. It was a political necessity. The carrying out of the sentence was mismanaged, but I was not to blame for that. I commanded the shooting, believing it necessary to save the lives of hundreds of others. There is no particle of self-reproach in my conscience for that act."

[On the gallows]

"I ask forgiveness of all men and forgive all mine enemies."

WANDERING SPIRIT, Cree War Chief

[Fort Battleford, Northwest Territories, Canada, November 27, 1885]

Found guilty of the murder of Indian Agent Thomas Quinn at Frog Lake, he went to the gallows with seven other participants in the massacre. The night before the execution, he made a speech.

"I wish to say good-bye to you all, officers as well as men. You have been good to me, better than I deserved. What I have done—that was bad. My punishment is no worse than I could expect. But let me tell you that I never thought to lift my hand against a white man. Years ago, when we lived on the plains and hunted the buffalo, I was a head warrior of the Crees in battle with the Blackfeet. I liked to fight. I took many scalps. But after you, the redcoats, came and the treaty was made with the white man, war was no more. I had never fought a white man. But lately we received bad advice. Of what good is it to speak of that now? I am sorry when it is too late. I only want to thank you, redcoats, and the sheriff, for your kindness. I am not afraid to die.

One thing only makes my heart beat with badness again! [Indicates ball and chain] *To be buried with that on my leg!* [Told it would be removed] *Then I will die satisfied. I may not be able in the morning, so now I say again to you all—good-bye! How! Aquisanee!"*

DIARY OF A GUNFIGHT

NATE CHAMPION, Cowboy
[Near Buffalo, Wyoming, April 9, 1892]

Accused of being a rustler in the Johnson County War, he created a remarkable and unique document—a journal of the dawn to dusk shootout in which he eventually died.

Me and Nick was getting breakfast when the attack took place. Two men was with us—Bill Jones and another man. The old man went after water and did not come back. His friend went to see what was the matter and he did not come back. Nick started out and I told him to look out, that I thought there was someone at the stable would not let them come back.

Nick is shot but not dead yet. He is awful sick. I must go and wait on him.

It is now about two hours since the first shot. Nick is still alive.

They are still shooting and are all around the house. Boys, there is bullets coming in like hail.

Them fellows is in such shape that I can't get at them. They are shooting from the stable and river and back of the house.

Nick is dead. He died about 9 o'clock. I see a smoke

down at the stable. I think they have fired it. I don't think they intend to let me get away this time.

It is now about noon. There is someone at the stable yet. They are throwing a rope at the door and dragging it back. I guess it is to draw me out. I wish that duck would go further so I can get a shot at him.

Boys, I don't know what they have done with them two fellows that stayed here last night.

Boys, I feel pretty lonesome just now. I wish there was someone here with me so we could watch all sides at once. They may fool around until I get a good shot before they leave.

It is about 3 o'clock now. There was a man in a buckboard and one on horseback just passed. They fired on them as they went by. I don't know if they killed them or not. I seen lots of men come out on horses on the other side of the river and take after them.

I shot at a man in the stable just now. Don't know if I got him or not. I must go look out again. It don't look as if there is much show of my getting away. I see twelve or fifteen men. One looks like [crossed out]. I don't know whether it is or not. I hope they did not catch them fellows that run over the bridge toward Smith's.

They are shooting at the house now. If I had a pair of glasses I believe I would know some of those men. They are coming back. I've got to look out.

Well, they have just got through shelling the house again like hail. I heard them splitting wood. I guess they are going to fire the house tonight. I think I will make a break when night comes, if alive.

Shooting again. I think they will fire the house this time.

It's not night yet. The house is all fired. Goodbye, boys, if I never see you again.

CONFESSIONS

KATIST-CHEN, "Swift Runner," Cree Brave
[Fort Saskatchewan, Northwest Territories, Canada, December 20, 1879]

At first insisting that his family died of starvation on a hunting trip, while waiting to be hanged for their murders, he suffered recurring nightmares and finally, three days before his execution, made a detailed confession to a priest who, in translating into English, changed Swift Runner's "windigo" into "the devil."

"We were camped in the woods about eight miles from here. In the beginning of winter we had not much to suffer. Game was plenty. I killed many moose and five or six bears; but about the middle of February I fell sick and to complete our misfortune those with me could find nothing to shoot. We had soon to kill our dogs and lived on their flesh while it lasted. Having recovered a little from my weakness, I traveled to a post of the Hudson's Bay Company on the Athabasca River and was assisted by the officer in charge, and returned to my camp with a small amount of provisions. That did not last us long. We all—that is, my mother, wife and six children (three boys and three girls) besides my brother and I—began to feel the pangs of hunger. My brother made up his mind to start with my mother in search of some game. I remained alone with my family.

Starvation became worse and worse. For many days we had nothing to eat. I advised my wife to start with the children and follow on the snow the tracks of my mother and brother, who perhaps had been lucky enough to kill a moose or a bear since they left us. For my part, though weak, I hoped that remaining alone I could support my life with my gun. All my family left me with the exception of a little boy, ten years of age.

I remained many days with my boy without finding any game and consequently without having a mouthful to eat. One morning I got up early and suddenly an abominable thought crossed my mind. My son was lying down close to the fire, fast asleep. Pushed by the evil spirits, I took my poor gun and shot him. The ball entered the top of his skull. Still he breathed. I began to cry. But what was the use? I then took my knife and sunk it twice into his side. Alas, he still breathed and I picked up a stick and killed him with it. I then satisfied my hunger by eating some of his flesh and lived on that for some days, extracting even the marrow from the bones.

For some days afterwards, I wandered through the woods. Unfortunately, I met my wife and children. I said to them that my son had died of starvation but I noticed immediately that they suspected the frightening reality.

They then told me that they had not seen either my mother or brother. No doubt both had died of starvation, otherwise they would have been heard of, as it is now seven months since then. Three days after joining my family, the oldest of my boys died. We dug a grave with an axe and buried him. We were then reduced to boiling some pieces of leather tent, our shoes and buffalo robes, in order to keep ourselves alive.

I discovered that my family wanted to leave me from fear of meeting the same fate as my boy. One morning I got up early, and I don't know why—I was mad. It seems to me that all the devils had entered my heart. My wife and chil-

*dren were asleep around me. Pushed by the evil spirit, I took
my gun, and placing the muzzle against her, shot her. I then
without delay took my hatchet and massacred my three little girls. There was now but only a little boy, seven years old,
surviving. I awoke him and told him to melt some snow for
water at once. The poor child was so weakened by long fast-
ing to make any refection of the frightful spectacle under his
eyes. I took the bodies of my little girls and cut them up. I
did the same with the corpse of my wife. I broke the skulls
and took out the brains, and broke up the bones in order to
get the marrow. My little son and I lived for seven or eight
days on the flesh—I eating the flesh of my wife and children, he the flesh of his mother and sisters.*

*At length I left there all the bones and started with the
last of my family. Snow began to melt now. Spring had commenced. Ducks arrived and flew every day around us, and I
could find enough to live upon, but I felt reluctant to see people. I then told my son that after some days we would meet
people; they will know very soon that I am a murderer, and
they will certainly make me die. As to you there is no fear;
say all you know; no harm will be done to you. One day I
had killed many ducks. I was a few miles from Egg Lake,
where some relations of mine lived. I was sitting at the camp
fire, when I told my son to go and fetch something five or six
paces off. At that moment the devil suddenly took possession
of my soul; and in order to live longer far from people, and
to put out of the way the only witness to my crimes, I seized
my gun and killed the last of my children and ate him as I
did the others. Some weeks after I was taken by the police,
sentenced to death, and in three days I am to be hanged."*

MITCH LEE, Outlaw
[Near Silver City, New Mexico, March 10, 1884]

Breaking jail with five others and wounded in the ensuing shootout, he was lynched by a posse who would not accept his persistent denials concerning a previous killing. Finally he realized that the mob would not relent.

"Well, by God! I did kill him."

MRS. KINGSTON, Former Madam
[Oklahoma City, Oklahoma, 1892]

On her deathbed, elderly Mrs. Kingston made a confession concerning the death of famed Pony Express rider Johnny Fry thirty years earlier.

"Shortly after I opened my resort—known as The Farm—in the early sixties, it was my custom to give a grand ball about once a month. They were attended by persons from hundreds of miles around.

We had a wonderful ballroom and a stable large enough to care for a hundred teams. Many times I have seen the stables full, and the balls would last from two days to a week.

One of the women at The Farm was an attractive Irish girl with many admirers, one of them a man by the name of Cleveland. He was known throughout the south and west as Cleveland the Outlaw.

He would nearly always drop in about midnight, would monopolize the company of this woman for a time, then would disappear and not be heard from until the next ball.

One night, Johnny Fry, down from St. Joseph, came in. He was immediately struck by the girl's appearance and looks, and he began dancing with her. The girl told Cleveland, when he showed up, that she already had a dancing partner, Fry.

Cleveland became sullen and sat in a corner with his

196

eyes on the dancing couple continuously. About 3:00 a.m. Fry excused himself from his companion and went outdoors. In a moment Cleveland followed.

Cleveland killed Johnny Fry between the back door of my kitchen and the barn, and strange as it may seem, I was the one who discovered the body. I called a big Negro man who was working for me, and together we carried the body into the basement.

The Negro dug a hole six feet deep and placed the body in the hole. He died very mysteriously a short time later, and that left me the sole possessor of the secret.

I have told you this as it occurred. If you have any doubts as to its truth and have interest enough, you may go to the old farm and dig in the basement. There you will find Johnny Fry's skeleton with a bullet through his skull."

SAM MARTIN, Outlaw
[Near Pawhuska, Indian Territory, August 3, 1903]

With his brother, he terrorized Indian Territory until shot down by a posse. In his dying moments, he showed some regret.

"I guess I have been on the wrong trail."

MRS. PETER HI-MA-DAN
[Hazelton, British Columbia, c. 1913]

On her deathbed she made a startling, but probably false, confession to a murder that her fugitive husband and Simon Gun-an-Noot were accused of.

"On that night I went to Two-Mile to get Peter. On the way there I met LeClair on the trail. He talked for a little while and then said bad things to me and wanted me to do bad things with him ... [After shooting him] I was beside the

197

trail crying, frightened at what I had done, when I heard another pony coming. It stopped and I looked up and saw Gun-an-Noot. He asked me why I was crying and I told him. He said for me to go home and forget it and he would tell people he had shot LeClair. He made me promise never to tell anybody. I went home. Gun-an-Noot took me there. He was going back to Two-Mile to kill McIntosh when his father came and said that McIntosh had been killed. His father said that everybody blamed him for shooting McIntosh."

DENIALS

J. W. ROVER, Miner
[Reno, Nevada, February 10, 1878]

After four trials, he was finally convicted of a three-year-old murder and brought to the gallows.

"Gentlemen: I have nothing much to say. I am so prostrated by this long persecution that I am unable to say what I should desire to, and the time, too, I suppose will not admit of it. I thought I was right and there is nothing that I know of, or that I have said, or thought, that was not right. ... I have done what I could in the matter and I consider that I have been unjustly treated. ... I never committed that crime. I arrived in California in the spring of '50; have been up and down in California and Nevada ever since, and I consider that I have been as instrumental and active as any living man that now walks the face of the earth in developing California to what she is today. Although I say it myself, I presume there is no credit to be placed to it, but my record will show that it is true, and I am not ashamed. If I have erred in this matter I did not know it. I do not know that I have any other redemption than being hung ... My aged parents are prostrated upon their backs at the news of that decision.

If there was anything positive produced in the preliminary examination I never had the pleasure of seeing it. But it is decided that I must hang, and I must suffer for another man's crime. I do say that it is cruel ... The charge was manufactured against me. It was a conspiracy, and all the evidence was placed to indict me, and was brought in and sworn to. I defy any one to show that I committed the crime, as God is my witness, and it was a manufactured job to defraud me out of my mine. This is the whole secret of it. If you call this law and justice this is a sad commentary. What have they done with my mine? They have allowed McWorthy to go on and work that mine, and ever since I have not received one picayune for it, and they have allowed him to go on and work the mine, and take the proceeds to Winnemucca and pay it to the State Attorney to convict Rover. What for? To defraud him out of the mine ... I and my counsel have done all we could. I do say this, that the trial at Winnemucca, of the case, was informal; it was irregular and illegal throughout."

[To his attorney, M. S. Bonnifield] *"Take my last love to Mrs. Bonnifield and her children ... I never did that, never committed that crime. Give my last love to those children.*

My God! Am I never to see those I love! Gentlemen, I will forgive you for this wrong that you have done. I will forgive you everything, and I ask forgiveness, gentlemen. I am not guilty of that crime. I am about to be sacrificed, although I did not commit it, and now I am about to atone for the blood and wickedness of another man and I cannot help it."

[To Sheriff Lamb] *Sheriff, go and do your duty, and get me out of this torture as soon as possible. Oh! I ask forgiveness from God."*

[As the trap is sprung] *"Oh, Lamb!"*

CECILIO LUCERO
[East Las Vegas, New Mexico, May 29, 1883]

Accused of murdering his cousin and another man, he was taken by a lynch mob.

"I did not do it! I did not kill them! The damned cowards that killed my cousin! I would like to kill them all!"

GEORGE BLACK, Murderer
[Laramie, Wyoming, February 26, 1890]

Although there were no witnesses to the murder of Ol' Tanglefoot Burnett, Black was convicted and hanged on the testimony of his partner, who confessed and was eventually released.

"No. I'm not the man that done the killing. That's all."

FLEMING "JIM" PARKER, Outlaw
[Prescott, Arizona, June 3, 1898]

Train robber and killer, Parker, on his execution day, wanted to take the time to inspect the scaffold.

"Hold on, boys, I want to look at this thing. I never looked at one before ... I have not much to say. I claim that I am getting something that ain't due me, but I guess every man who is about to be hanged says the same thing, so that don't cut no figure. Whenever the people says I must go, I am the one who can go and make no kick ... Hold on, I want to shake hands with the boys ... Tell the boys I died game and like a man...Don't get excited. George, you put her [the hood] on ... It's too tight."

NEWTON ANDREWS, Murderer
[Canon City, Colorado, June 16, 1905]

He made his final speech from the gallows, where he was executed for a pointless murder committed with Frederick Arnold.

> *"Gentlemen, I am no speaker; I don't know how to make a speech, but in another moment I'll be dead. You people know I'm going to tell you the truth because I'm going to die ... I was too drunk to realize what Arnold was going to do. I was pushed into the house and the next thing I knew the shooting began. I took my gun and shot the roof... May God forgive me for ever having started to drink, but He knows I intended no harm when I went into Mrs. Youngblood's house."*

FREDERICK ARNOLD, Murderer
[Canon City, Colorado, June 16, 1905]

The youngest man legally executed in Colorado made a friend in prison—the warden's son, who witnessed the hanging.

> *"Only this, I never was given a fair chance and I am innocent of this murder. This is simple murder by the state of Colorado ... Goodbye, Billy."*

EMILIO "EMPEROR PIC" PICARIELLO, Bootlegger
[Fort Saskatchewan, Alberta, May 2, 1923]

On the scaffold for his part in the murder of an Alberta provincial police officer.

> *"You are hanging an innocent man. God help me."*

FLORENCE LASSANDRA
[Fort Saskatchewan, Alberta, May 2, 1923]

Picariello's companion, she fired the shot that killed an Alberta provincial police officer.

"Why do you hang me when I didn't do anything? Is there no one here who has any pity? I forgive everybody."

INNOCENT BYSTANDERS

ELIZABETH HASTINGS
[Palmdale, California, June 1875]

The twenty-year-old woman was killed by gunshot when she interrupted a bank robbery being performed by an intoxicated hardcase who needed five hundred dollars to get back into a poker game down the street.

"A holdup! A holdup!"

JAMES MALONE, Farmer
[Winona, Minnesota, July 29, 1879]

The night before he died he gave a statement to authorities, in the presence of a suspect, about a drunken encounter in French Lou's bordello, where he was shot from behind.

"Ed Lawlor did not shoot me. He was present when the shooting occurred. The man present walked past me and hit me as he passed. I had just drunk a glass of beer and threw the glass at him after he hit me. I saw a revolver in the man's hand and turned and ran. I heard a shot fired. It hit me. I then heard another and it struck me in the back of the head. When I heard the report of the revolver first I was just

out of the door. When I was hit the second time I was about fifteen feet from the door. I think he had the revolver in his hand when he hit me; he struck me an awful blow. I am positive that this is the man ... that had the revolver."

DEL SIMMONS
[Ingalls, Oklahoma Territory, September 1, 1893]

Asked by a lawman to identify an approaching horseman, Simmons' last words and pointing finger sparked the famous gunbattle between lawmen and the Doolin gang. The fourteen-year-old Simmons was shot as he ran for cover.

"Why, that's Bitter Creek!"

J. W. MITCHELL, Barber
[Chandler, Oklahoma Territory, July 30, 1894]

Sitting outside his shop, he uttered the warning that brought him instant death from members of the Bill Cook–Cherokee Bill gang, who were in front of the bank.

"Robbers are in town!"

JAMES H. LEWIS
[Near Cloud Chief, Oklahoma, September 1, 1910]

After a lifetime of being on the wrong side of the law, Lewis settled down at the home of his daughter, generally minding his own business until an argument occurred between his son-in-law and his son. As Lewis' son threatened to kill the son-in-law, Lewis interjected his last bit of advice, which drew the anger and the fire of the incensed son.

"Aw, you shouldn't do that."

SHOWDOWNS

EDWARD SHORT, Deputy Marshal
[Waukomis, Oklahoma Territory, August 23, 1891]

As the train neared town, he shot to death prisoner Black-Faced Charley Bryant, who had desperately snatched a revolver and shot Short.

"The damn bastard got me, Jim, but I got him. I wish I could see Mother."

"BLACK-FACED" CHARLEY BRYANT, Outlaw
[Waukomis, Oklahoma Territory, August 23, 1891]

As he was being transported by train, he tried to escape custody and was shot by Deputy Short.

"Please pull my boots off, and don't tell the folks back home."

W. C. McDANIEL, Deputy Marshal
[Near Coffeyville, Kansas, March 13, 1895]

Attempting to arrest Bob Rogers, McDaniel went up the stairs and offered Rogers a chance to surrender.

"Drop those guns!"

BOB ROGERS, Outlaw
[Near Coffeyville, Kansas, March 13, 1895]

After killing Deputy McDaniels and then offering to surrender, Rogers came out, rifle lowered, but, perhaps reacting to the law-men's callous reply ("We don't need one"), he seemed to change his mind and raised the rifle, provoking gunfire.

"Do you have a warrant for me?"

JIM McKINNEY, Outlaw
[Bakersfield, California, April 19, 1903]

The long-time badman was trapped in a friend's room by law-men, two of whom died in the famous shootout, their moment of injury prompting McKinney's last comments before a shotgun blast hit him in the face.

"There goes old four eyes . . .
There goes old Overall. Let's get Tower."

WILLIAM TIBBET, Deputy
[Bakersfield, California, April 19, 1903]

With other lawmen attempting to capture outlaw Jim McKinney, who was hiding in the room of his friend Al Hulse, Tibbet approached the door and made an inquiry, only to be met with a volley of buckshot and bullets. He died shortly after.

"Hulse shot me ... I have made my peace with God...I am dying. I am suffering terribly. I can't stand it."

ASSASSINS

ROBERT FORD, Saloon Owner
[Creed, Colorado, June 8, 1892]

Moments before Ed O'Kelley shotgunned him in his saloon, Ford, notorious as the killer of Jesse James, saw on a charity list that Soapy Smith had donated five dollars.

"I'll raise him five."

[Then he wrote] *"Bob Ford—Ten Dollars—Charity covereth a multitude of sins."*

EDWARD CAPEHART O'KELLEY
[Oklahoma City, Oklahoma, January 13, 1904]

Insisting upon carrying a gun, the man who killed Jesse James' assassin was often arrested and finally attacked Officer Burnett, who eventually shot him.

"You come with me. I'll arrest you, you son of a bitch. "

[To a friend, during the fight] *"We will murder this fellow!"*

TOM HORN, Hired Gun
[Cheyenne, Wyoming, November 20, 1903]

Hired by the cattle barons to put a stop to rustling, he was sentenced to hang for murdering fourteen-year-old Willie Nickell. The trap door on the gallows was operated by the weight of water.

[Seeing a row of officers] *"Ed, that's the sickest looking lot of damned sheriffs I ever seen."*

[Waiting for the running water to spring the trap] *"What's the matter? Getting nervous I might tip over?"*

[Waiting while water runs] *"Joe, they tell me you're married now. I hope you're doing well. Treat her right."*

"KILLIN'" JIM MILLER, Hired Killer
[Ada, Oklahoma, April 19, 1909]

Perhaps the deadliest killer of the West, he was hanged by a lynch mob, meeting death as casually as he administered it to others.

"Just let the record show that I've killed fifty-one men . . . I'd like to have my coat. I don't want to die naked . . . If I can't have my coat, then how about my hat? . . . I'm ready now; you couldn't kill me otherwise. Let 'er rip!"

SUICIDES

RICHARD A. BARTER, Outlaw
"Rattlesnake Dick"
[Near Auburn, California, July 11, 1859]

Shot up by a posse, he was later found dead, perhaps having committed suicide. He left a note referring to a relentless lawman whom he mistakenly thought he had shot during his escape.

"Rattlesnake Dick dies, but never surrenders, as all true Britons do. If J. Boggs is dead, I am satisfied."

J. K. LYON, Judge
[El Paso, Texas, April 20, 1895]

Implicated with Constable Schoonmaker in a scheme to collect illegal fines, he at first denied the accusation, then committed suicide, leaving this note.

"I expect to be within the presence of my God and Maker within thirty minutes; and I make this statement that I have not directly nor indirectly been connected with Jim Schoonmaker or any of his unlawful acts—so help me God as a Royal Arch Mason."

THOMAS SPENCER HARRIS, Pioneer Printer/Journalist
[Tulare, California, 1893]

After roaming from mining camp to mining camp initiating newspapers or editing existing ones without much financial success, he eventually ended up in poverty, consoling himself with alcohol until his suicide by gunshot.

> [Suicide note] *"I have had a great time. Never mind what may be said. Many people say what they think they know. But they will know more as they grow older. But what is the use of knowledge when it comes into contact with brains cultivated by years of experience. I devote my brains ... help yourself to what is left. T. S. Harris"*

ANNIE JAMES, Prostitute
[Silverton, Colorado, March 26, 1897]

Like many other soiled doves, she committed suicide by drinking carbolic acid, suffering for three hours before dying. Her suicide note hints at the hard life she was enduring.

> *"I can't stand your abuse any longer, good bye. Annie."*

PATRICK CASEY, Saloon Owner
[Deadwood, South Dakota, May 1897]

Depressed by lack of family, money, and friends, Casey invited two friends to have a drink, took a revolver from under the counter, and shot himself twice in the chest.

> *"Good-bye, boys, I am going to kill myself!"*

> [Shoots] *"That didn't hurt a bit."*

> [To the friends who tried to disarm him]
> *"Get out or I'll kill you!"*

JAMES YOUNGER, Reformed Outlaw
[St. Paul, Minnesota, October 18, 1902]

One of the famous Younger brothers, Jim, after serving his prison sentence, depressed, unable to begin a new life, wrote a letter and then, just before shooting himself in the head, added his last words on the envelope.

"Oct. 18. Last night on earth. So good by Lassie, for I shall think of thee. Forgive me for this is the only chance. I have done nothing wrong.

But politics is all that Van Sant, Wolfer and others of their stripe, care for. Let the people judge. Treat me fair reporters for I am a square fellow, a socialist and decidedly in favor of Woman Rights.

Bryan is the brightest man these United States ever produced. His one mistake was not coming out for all the people and absolute socialism. Come out Bryan. There is no such thing as a personal God. God is universal and I know him well and I am not afraid.

I have no pity for the pardoning board. They do not stop to consider their wives or to think of the man who knows how to love and appreciate a friend in truth. Good-bye, sweet Lassie.

Jim Younger"

[On envelope] *"To all that is good and true I love and bid farewell. Jim Younger."*

[On other side of envelope] *"Oh, Lassie, Goodbye. All relatives just stay away from me. No crocodile tears wanted. Reporters: Be my friends. Burn me up."*

HARVEY LOGAN, "Kid Curry," Outlaw
[Near Rifle, Colorado, June 7, 1904]

Pursued by a posse, wounded, he opted for suicide just after a gang member asked him if he were hit.

"Yes, and I'm going to end it here."

AL HULSE, Prisoner
[Bakersfield, California, October 15, 1906]

Languishing in jail for years while appealing conviction for his part in the shooting deaths of Will Tibbet and Jeff Packard in April 1903, he began suffering mental disturbances, finally slitting his throat with a razor after these comments to his fellow prisoners.

"Thank you for all you have done for me.
It is all off with me today."

ELBERT "EB" BASSETT, Cowboy
[Near Craig, Colorado, November 19, 1925]

Haunted nightly by the face of a man he helped lynch in 1898, this tight-lipped cowboy gave no indication in his suicide note that he was under additional strain because of financial problems and rustling accusations.

"No one but me knew or suspected what I was going to do,
no one. Eb Bassett."

TOM ROSS, Ranch Foreman
[Blackfoot Indian Reservation, Montana, February 3, 1929]

Having escaped from Huntsville Prison in Texas, where he had committed murder, he worked under the alias of Charles Gannon as a ranch foreman until he committed suicide, leaving a note after shooting the ranch inspector who found fault with his management of the property.

"To the Public: This fellow was new in the cow business. He might have been o.k. among a bunch of Dagoes but not cowpunchers. Goodbye to the world. Charles Gannon."

GLENN HIBBS, Cowboy
[Near Winnemucca, Nevada, October 7, 1933]

Recently divorced, he returned to the Pinson ranch, where he threatened his former wife, shot Sheriff Lamb, and then committed suicide, leaving a farewell note on a rifle-shell box for his five-year-old daughter.

"To Jo Hibbs. I come to the Pinson Ranch to visit you peaceably. Your mother and your aunt tried to shoot me and did run me away. What will happen now I do not know. I am not responsible for what does so goodby my sweetheart. Glenn Hibbs."

DYING ADVICE

GEORGE PIERSON, Saloon Owner
[Boise, Idaho, August 1, 1884]

Coming home to find a former friend attacking his common-law wife, Pierson chased the assailant and killed him, Pierson's relentless pursuit earning him a trip to the gallows.

> *"I am about to suffer the extreme penalty of the law, not because of the crime, but because of prejudice caused by my running away from jail last summer . . . I warn you, my fellow citizens, against the practice of carrying arms. It is a bad one, and causes many crimes to be committed. . . . In all my dealings with Johnny I did what I thought was right by a fellow man. If I had had justice I would not be here. A man's home is his castle."*

BOOD CRUMPTON, Murderer
[Fort Smith, Arkansas, June 30, 1891]

On the gallows, he paid the penalty for killing his companion during a drinking bout.

"To all you who are present, especially you young men—the next time you are about to take a drink of whisky, look closely into the bottom of the glass and see if you cannot observe in there a hangman's noose."

JOHN MOSHIK, Murderer
[Minneapolis, Minnesota, March 18, 1898]

On the gallows for murder, he was intent on giving his executioners instructions to improve their efficiency.

"You haven't got the rope tight enough about my neck ... My legs ... my feet."

THOMAS "BLACK JACK" KETCHUM, Outlaw
[Clayton, New Mexico, April 25, 1901]

On the day of his execution, he wrote some advice to other would-be outlaws.

"My advice to the boys of the country is not to steal horses and sheep, but either rob a train or a bank when you have got to be an outlaw, and every man who comes in your way, kill him; spare him no mercy, for he will show you none. This is the way I feel about it, and I think I feel right about it."

Later that day, his last words took on posthumous irony when the rope sliced through his neck, severing his head from his body.

"The rope looks like a good one ... Goodbye, please dig my grave very deep ... All right, hurry up ... Ready. Let 'er go."

LOVERS' QUARREL

WILLIAM A. GARLAND, Hop Fiend
[Clifton, Arizona, January 28, 1903]

Quarreling with his lover, China Dot, the opium-addicted Garland decided to end the relationship by killing her and then shooting himself.

"Dot, I think I'll kill you."

FLORA QUICK, "Tom King," Horse Thief
[Clifton, Arizona, January 28, 1903]

After years of horse stealing as "Tom King," the Oklahoman drifted to Arizona, where, as China Dot, opium addict, she was shot by her angry lover, William Garland.

"All right. Go ahead."

J. A. TRACY, Mine Agent
[Mescal Station, Arizona, February 28, 1907]

A frustrated lover, at Benson, Arizona, train station he drew a pistol on his paramour and her new "husband" but became involved in a spectacular shootout with Arizona Ranger Wheeler, who wounded him so badly he was immediately taken aboard the train to Tucson.

"There is a woman in the case."

POETS

JERRY CRAINE

[Coloma, California, October 26, 1855]

After killing his lover, Susan Newnham, he botched the suicide
part of the plan but eventually made his way to the gallows,
where he and Mickey Free sang Craine's composition to a crowd
of over five thousand.

"Come friends and all others I bid you adieu,
The gates are open to welcome us through,
No valleys or shadow do I see on the road,
For the angels are waiting to take me to God.
My body no longer my spirit shall claim,
This day I am going from sorrow and pain,
The necklace and gallows will soon set me free,
Then Oh how joyous and happy my spirit shall be.
Then millions and millions of ages may roll,
Progression be ever the theme of my soul;
To beauty and grandeur I ever be wed,
And worlds without number my spirit will tread.
Ye worldlings and Christians may sneer or may frown,
Your unfounded systems are fast tumbling down,
And sadness and sorrow will give way to mirth,
And peace and good will shall extend o'er the earth!

Come brothers and sisters, a long, long farewell—
The way it is clear, I can see it quite well—
No valleys or shadows I see on the road,
But angels are waiting to take me to God!
I'm going, I'm going, to the land of the free,
Where all love each other, and ever agree;
I'm going, I'm going, I'm going, I'm gone!
Oh, friends and relations, 'tis done, it is done."

"Susan, receive me. I will soon be with you."

MICKEY FREE, Murderer
[Coloma, California, October 26, 1855]

On the gallows, he and Jerry Craine entertained a huge crowd by singing Craine's song.

"Now, boys, see that this is done up right."

RUFUS BUCK, Outlaw
[Fort Smith, Arkansas, July 1, 1896]

After Buck's gang terrorized Indian Territory, killing, robbing, and raping, Buck went to the gallows leaving this poem in his cell.

MY dreAm,—1896
I, dreamP'T, I, wAs, in, HeAven,
Among, The, AngeLs, Fair;
i'd, neAr, seen, none, so HAndsome,
THAT, TWine, in, goLden, Hair;
THey, Looked, so, neAT, And, SAng, so, sweet,
And, PLAY,d THe, THe, goLden, HArp,
i, wAs, ABout, To, Pick, An, AngeL, ouT,
And, TAke, Her, To, mY, HeArT;
BuT, The, momenT, i, BegAn, To, PleA,
i, THougHT, oF, You, mY, Love,

THere, wAs, none, i'd, seen, so, BeAuTiFuLL,
On, eArTH, or, HeAven, ABove,
gooD, By, My, Dear, Wife, anD. MoTHer
                         all.so.My. sisTers

           RUFUS, BUCK
           Youse. Truly

I Day. of. July
Tu, The, Yeore
   Off
   1896

                           H
                           O
                           L
                           Y
              FATHer   Son
                           g
                           H
                           O
                           S
                           T
              Virtue & resurresur.rection.

RememBer, Me, ROCK, OF, Ages:

222

CHAUNCEY THOMAS, Writer
[Denver, Colorado, September, 1941]

Author of stories set in the Rocky Mountains, where he was born, expert on firearms, the Sage of the Rockies fired his final bullet into his own brain, leaving behind plans for his burial monument and his epitaph.

> *Traveler on this summit rest,*
> *Behold the peaks two oceans breast,*
> *Then on this grave lay you a stone,*
> *A Mountain Man sleeps here alone.*

QUIET END TO AN ADVENTUROUS LIFE

ZEKE PROCTOR
[Near Watts, Oklahoma, February 28, 1907]

The half-white, half-Cherokee Civil War veteran lived a dangerous life on both sides of the law, finishing his long career as a
Deputy U.S. Marshal. He died at the age of seventy-six of pneumonia, apparently concerned about several outlaws whom he
had given refuge in his barn.

"Feed the boys good."

CARRY NATION, Prohibitionist
[Leavenworth, Kansas, June 2, 1911]

The hatchet-wielding saloon-smasher died quietly in a hospital,
interrupted by death as she started to lecture her doctor on his
addiction to tobacco.

"I have done what I could ..."

ANDREW "HECK" THOMAS, Frontier Marshal
[Lawton, Oklahoma, August 15, 1912]

One of the "Three Guardsmen" along with Bill Tilghman and Chris Madsen, the legendary Oklahoma lawman survived a lifetime of dangerous encounters because he always made his arrest before producing the warrant. He died quietly at home six days after writing a no-nonsense note to his long-time friend and fellow lawman Chris Madsen.

"This malady is troubling me again, and I know I have not the strength to resist it, so no matter what happens don't you and Bill come down here, and no flowers. . . . No need to answer, for I will not be alive to receive it. Remember me to your children and good-bye forever. Your friend, Heck."

WILLIAM FREDERICK CODY, "Buffalo Bill," Showman
[Denver, Colorado, January 10, 1917]

The famous showman, scout, and buffalo hunter who brought the Wild West to large audiences in the East and in Europe, died quietly. Fully aware in his last two days that he was dying, he hoped to see his foster son one more time.

"Let's forget about it and play high five . . . I wish Johnny would come."

WILLIAM WESLEY VAN ORSDEL, Methodist Circuit Rider
[Great Falls, Montana, December 19, 1919]

After a lifetime of preaching the gospel in the communities of Montana and Idaho, Brother Van suffered a stroke and fell into a coma, from which he awoke shortly before he died.

"I haven't an enemy. Only friends. Tell the people of Montana that I love them all."

225

WILLIAM B. "BAT" MASTERSON, Reporter
[New York, New York, October 21, 1921]

The famous former buffalo hunter, lawman, and gambler ended his legendary career as a sports reporter for the *New York Telegraph,* speaking his last words in response to a fellow worker's query about his health; then, victim of a heart attack, he slumped over upon his last written words, his final sports column.

"All right."

[Written] *"Lew Tendler received a little more than $12,000 for his scrap with Rocky Kansas at the Garden a week ago. Not so bad for a job like that ... No wonder these birds are flying high when they get that kind of money for an hour's work. Just think of an honest, hard-working farmer laboring from daylight to dark for forty years of his life, and lucky if he finishes with as much as one of these birds gets in an hour. Yet there are those who argue that everything breaks even in this old dump of a world of ours.*

I suppose these ginks who argue that way hold that because the rich man gets ice in the summer and the poor man gets it in the winter things are breaking even for both. Maybe so, but I'll swear I can't see it that way."

WYATT EARP, Frontier Lawman
[Los Angeles, California, January 13, 1929]

The famous lawman, gambler, and mine speculator died in bed at his home at the age of eighty-one. After a life of adventure in Dodge City and Tombstone, he succumbed to chronic cystitis. On his last day, about seven in the morning, he awoke and, moments before he died, said,

"Suppose, suppose..."

YELLOW WOLF, Nez Perce Warrior
[Near Colville, Washington, August 21, 1935]

Nephew of Chief Joseph, and one of the leaders in the Nez Perce retreat of 1877, he died quietly on the reservation.

"I am now going! My old friends have come for me! They are here! Do you not see them? There stands Eshawis, and there Peopee Howisthowit, and Diskoskow. They have come to take me to Ahkunkenekoo."

COLONEL FRANK MEYER
[Fairplay, Colorado, February 12, 1954]

Once a thirteen-year-old drummer boy in the Civil War, the former buffalo hunter spoke to his nurse, then slipped into a coma three months short of his 104th birthday.

"I'm the last of the hide hunters left alive."

BIBLIOGRAPHY

See Index for Reference Numbers

"American Indian Gallery," *Old West*, Summer 1966. [A0]

Anderson, Frank W., *Hanging In Canada*, Surrey, Heritage House Publishing Company Ltd., 1982. [A1]

———, *Oldtime Western Sheriffs and Outlaws*, Vol. 1, Saskatoon, Frank W. Anderson, Publisher. [A2]

———, *Sheriffs and Outlaws of Western Canada*, Calgary, Frontier Publishing Ltd., 1973. [A3]

Arnold, George, "El Dorado Showdown," *True West*, March 1994. [A4]

Askins, Charles, Texans, *Guns & History*, New York, Winchester Press, 1970. [A5]

Ballard, David M., "Yellow Wolf, Loner in the Nez Perce War," *Frontier Times*, April 1985. [B0]

———, "War of Extermination Backfired," *Wild West*, June 1989. [B1]

Battle Mountain Messenger, February 23, 1878, Battle Mountain, Nevada. [B2]

Bartholomew, Ed, *Wild Bill Longley: A Texas Hardcase*, Houston, The Frontier Press of Texas, 1953. [B3]

Barton, Barbara, "Battle at Dove Creek," *Old West*, Winter 1994. [B4]

Bate, W. N., "Frontier Legend," *Old West*, Spring 1972. [B5]

Baum, Jim, "Colorado City Killings," *Old West*, Winter 1988. [B6]

Bentz, Donald N., " Invitation To A Hanging," *Western Frontier*, May 1985. [B7]

Berk, Lee, "A Tough Nevada Lawman," *True West*, January 1983. [B8]

Berton, Pierre, *The National Dream*, Toronto, McClelland & Stewart Ltd., 1972. [B9]

———, *The Wild Frontier*, Toronto, McClelland & Stewart Ltd., 1978. [B10]

Bird, Allan G., *Bordellos of Blair Street,* Grand Rapids, The Other Shop, 1987. [B11]

Boessenecker, John, *Badge and Buckshot,* Norman, University of Oklahoma Press, 1988. [B12]

———, "William Wells' Bloody Escape," *True West,* September 1986. [B13]

Bordigon, Maxine G., "Warriors & Chiefs," *Wild West,* October 1991. [B14]

Bowsfield, Hartwell, *Louis Riel: The Rebel and the Hero,* Toronto, Oxford University Press, 1971. [B15]

Braly, David, "A Night of Murders in Old Prineville," *True West,* December 1997. [B16]

Brant, Marley, *The Outlaw Youngers,* Lanham, Madison Books, 1992. [B17]

Breihan, Carl W., "The Day Sam Bass Was Killed," *Real West,* May 1975. [B18]

Brooks, Juanita, *The Mountain Meadows Massacre,* Norman, University of Oklahoma Press, 1985. [B19]

Brown, Larry K., "Dinner With The Devil," *NOLA Quarterly,* Vol. XX, No. 3, July–Sept., 1996. [B20]

———,"The Fine Art of Murder," *True West,* May 1998. [B21]

———,"Fingered by the Fire," *NOLA Quarterly,* Vol. XIX, No. 4, Oct.–Dec., 1995. [B22]

———,"Just Ice," *True West,* June 1997. [B23]

———,"Look At Me!...I Die Brave!," *True West,* December 1995. [B24]

Browning, James A., and Dave Johnson, "A Feudist By Any Other Name," *NOLA Quarterly,* Vol. XVIII, No. 3, July–Sept., 1994. [B25]

Bryan, Howard, *Robbers, Rogues and Ruffians,* Santa Fe, Clear Light Publishers, 1991. [B26]

———, *Wildest of The Wild West,* Santa Fe, Clear Light Publishers, 1988. [B27]

Buchanan, Bob, "Truly Western," *True West,* May 1984. [B28]

Burchfield, Chris, "Murder at Industry Bar," *True West,* March 1996. [B29]

Burns, Walter Noble, *The Saga of Billy the Kid,* New York, Konecky & Konecky, 1992. [B30]

Burr, Wesley H., "Discovered in 1887, The Thoen Stone 'Documents' A June 1834 Tragedy in The Black Hills," *Wild West,* April 1997. [B31]

Burton, Art, *Black, Red, and Deadly,* Austin, Eakin Press, 1991. [B32]

Burton, Art T., "Murder of an Oklahoma Marshal," *Old West,* Spring 1993. [B33]

Burton, Jeff, " 'A Great Man Hunt'—Correspondence From 'W.B.S.'," London, *The English Westerners' Brand Book,* 1975-76. [B34]

Carroll, Murray L., "As an Outlaw and Escape Artist Dan Bogan Was the Real McCoy," *WOLA Journal,* Vol. II, No. 1, Spring-Summer 1992. [C0]

Chegwyn, Michael, "One Killing Too Many," *True West,* November 1991. [C1]

Cheyenne Daily Sun, April 10, 1877. [C2]

Chicoine, B. Paul, "Hense Wiseman's Revenge," *Real West,* November 1979. [C3]

Chrisman, Harry E., *The Ladder of Rivers,* Denver, Sage Books, 1962. [C4]

Clark, Robert A., ed., *The Killing of Chief Crazy Horse,* Lincoln, Bison Books, University of Nebraska Press, 1988. [C5]

Cline, Don, "Did Billy-the-Kid Kill Frank Cahill?" *NOLA Quarterly,* Vol. X, No. 3, Winter 1986. [C6]

―――, "Frank Over The Fence," *True West,* September 1998. [C7]

Cline, Donald, "Cole Young, Train Robber," *Old West,* Summer 1985. [C8]

Cloud, Jim, "Dead: The Man, Who Killed the Man, Who Killed Jesse James," *Oklahombres,* Vol. III, No. 3, Spring 1992. [C9]

Coburn, Walt, "Dual Hanging in Arizona," *Badman,* Vol. 1, No. 1, 1971. [C10]

Connell, Evan S., *Son of the Morning Star,* San Francisco, North Point Press, 1984. [C11]

Conway, Lenore and James D. Horan, "Tiburcio Vasquez: Long Career for Notorious California Bandit," *NOLA Quarterly,* Vol. XII, No. 4, Spring 1988. [C12]

Cook, D. J., *Hands Up!,* Norman, University of Oklahoma Press, 1958. [C13]

Copps, Benjamin, *The Great Chiefs,* Alexandria, Time-Life Books, 1981. [C14]

Corless, Hank, "Cherokee Bob's Last Gunfight," *Old West,* Spring 1988. [C15]

Cornish, Ken, "Mad Dog Dilda," *Old West,* Spring 1972. [C16]

Corum, Michael, "Double Hanging In Coloma," *Wild West,* December 1996. [C17]

Cude, Elton R., *The Free and Wild Dukedom of Bexar,* San Antonio, Munguia Printers, 1978. [C18]

Davis, Harold Redd, "California's Longest Manhunt," *Old West,* Fall 1984. [D1]

DeArment, Robert K., "Bad Month for Badmen," *True West,* August 1990. [D2]

―――, *Bat Masterson,* Norman, University of Oklahoma Press, 1980. [D3]

―――, "The Blood-spattered Trail of Milton J. Yarberry," *Old West,* Fall 1985. [D4]

————, "Bloody Easter," *Old West,* Spring 1994. [D5]

————, *George Scarborough,* Norman, University of Oklahoma Press, 1992. [D6]

————, "Jeff Kidder, Arizona Ranger," *NOLA Quarterly,* Vol. VII, No. 4, Winter 1982-83. [D7]

————, "John Larn's Bloody Trail Drive," *True West,* January 1997. [D8]

————, *Knights of the Green Cloth,* Norman, University of Oklahoma Press, 1990. [D9]

————, "Kreeger's Toughest Arrest," *True West,* June 1986. [D10]

d'Easum, Dick, *Fragments of Villainy,* Boise, Statesman Printing Company, 1959. [D11]

Dedera, Don, *A Little War of Our Own,* Flagstaff, Northland Press, 1988. [D12]

DeMattos, Jack, "Black Jack Ketchum," *Real West,* June 1984. [D13]

Dimsdale, Thomas J., *The Vigilantes of Montana,* Norman, University of Oklahoma Press, 1985. [D14]

Dixon, Dick, "Blown To Pieces By Seven Shots," *Real West,* June 1987. [D15]

Dixon, Madoline C., "The Inseparables," *True West,* June 1988. [D16]

Dobie, J. Frank, " 'His Looks And My Ways Would Kill Any Man' ," *Old West,* Winter 1965. [D17]

Doctor, Joseph E., *Shotguns on Sunday,* Bakersfield, Bakersfield Advertising Club, 1975. [D18]

Dodge, Matt, "Jim Parker: Good Cowboy Gone Bad?," *Real West,* July 1980. [D19]

————, "The Lynchers," *Real West,* August 1983. [D20]

————, "The Vigilantes: Nebraska's Public Defenders," *Real West,* October 1984. [D21]

Drago, Harry Sinclair, The Great Range Wars, Lincoln, University of Nebraska Press, 1970. [D22]

Dugan, Mark, *Tales Never Told Around the Campfire,* Athens, Swallow Press/Ohio University Press, 1992. [D23]

Eckhart, Jerry, "Rath City: Texas Hide Town," *True West,* September 1992. [E1]

Edwards, Harold L., "'By The Rope Route' ," *Real West,* November 1987. [E2]

————, "A Point of Honor," *True West,* November 1993. [E3]

————, "Shootout on Number 19," *True West,* May 1987. [E4]

————, "Tragedy at Mussel Slough," *Old West,* Winter 1992. [E5]

————, "The Twisted Trail of Billy Stiles," *True West,* November 1994. [E6]

————, "Who Killed William Tibbet?," *Real West,* June 1987. [E7]

Engebretson, Doug, "Dick Burnett," *Real West,* June 1986. [E8]

————, *Empty Saddles, Forgotten Names,* Aberdeen, North Plains Press, 1982. [E9]

Espy, Watt, "Quadruple Hanging at Missoula, Montana," *NOLA Quarterly,* Vol. IV, No. 3, March 1979. [E10]

Evans, R. G., *Murder On the Plains,* Aldergrove, Frontier Publishing Ltd., 1968. [E11]

Ewing, William E., "Mail Carrier's Last Ride," *Old West,* Fall 1988. [E12]

Farnsworth, Janet, "The Power Brothers Shootout," *True West,* December 1992. [F0]

Fehrenbach, T. R., *Lone Star,* New York, Collier Books, MacMillan Publishing Company, 1980. [F1]

Fitterer, Gary P., "Braddock and Moore," *True West,* December 1999. [F2]

Fleek, Sherman L., "Exodus Triggered By Assassins," *Wild West,* October 1988. [F3]

————, "Gunfighters & Lawmen," *Wild West,* April 1989. [F4]

Florin, Lambert, *Boot Hill,* New York, Bonanza Books, Crown Publishers, 1966. [F5]

————, *Tales the Western Tombstones Tell,* New York, Bonanza Books, Crown Publishers, 1967. [F6]

Foster, Robert L., "A Lawless Land," *True West,* September 1988. [F7]

Freeman, G. D., *Midnight and Noonday,* ed. Richard L. Lane, Norman, University of Oklahoma Press, 1984. [F8]

Fugleberg, Paul, "Brother Van: A Diamond in the Rough," *True West,* August 1989. [F9]

Galey, John, "Gunfighters & Lawmen," *Wild West,* June 1988. [G1]

Gardiner, George, "Gunfighters and Lawmen," *Wild West,* June 1998. [G2]

Garrigues, George L., "Convicts on the Loose," *Wild West,* October 1998. [G3]

George, Wally, "Tequila and Gunpowder," *True West,* December 1958. [G4]

Gilfert, Shirley, "Nebraska City Mobocracy," *Old West,* Summer 1990. [G5]

Gilstrap, Lou, "Peacemakers Walk A Dangerous Road," *Old West,* Fall 1973. [G6]

Gray, Frank S., "Three Killed in a Drunken Brawl," *Frontier Times,* January 1980. [G7]

Green, Ford, "Those Thousand Colts That Went to War," *True West,* October 1979. [G8]

Hafen, Mary Ann, "Memories of a Handcart Pioneer," *Let Them Speak for Themselves,* ed. Christiane Fischer, Hamden, Archon Books, The Shoe String Press, Inc., 1977. [H0]

Haines, Joe D., Jr., "The Haines Brothers Volunteer," *True West,* September 1982. [H1]

————, "Wiley Haines Was A Courageous Lawman," *NOLA Quarterly,* Vol. VIII, No. 1, Spring 1983. [H2]

Hamilton, Douglas, "In Pursuit of The Flying Dutchman," *Old West,* Summer 1990. [H3]

Hanna, Wilma Colson, "Great Chief of the Choctaws," *Western Frontier,* November 1985. [H4]

Harrison, Fred, "Innocent and Hanged," *Western Frontier,* May 1986. [H5]

Hart, Will, "The Daly Gang's Reign of Terror," *Wild West,* June 1995. [H6]

Hartman, Mary, and Elmo Ingenthron, *Bald Knobbers,* Gretna, Pelican Publishing Company, 1988. [H7]

Hawkes, John, *Saskatchewan and Its People,* Vol. I, Chicago/Regina, The S. J. Clarke Publishing Company, 1924. [H8]

Hegne, Barbara, *Border Outlaws of Montana,* North Dakota & Canada, Eagle Point, Hegne, 1993. [H9]

Hennigh, Larry, "By Invitation Only," *True West,* April 1993. [H10]

Herberg, Ruth, "Nine Died: Three Lived," *Old West,* Fall 1973. [H11]

Herring, Edward, "Gunfight at Spokogee," *Wild West,* April 1997. [H12]

Holbrook, Marion R., "Riverbank Massacre," *True West,* September 1982. [H13]

Holden, Jan, "Carry Nation Your Loving Home Defender," *Old West,* Spring 1999. [H14]

Horan, James D., *The Gunfighters: The Authentic Wild West,* New York, Crown Publishers Inc., 1976. [H15]

——, *The Lawmen: The Authentic Wild West,* New York, Crown Publishers, Inc., 1980. [H16]

——, *The Outlaws: The Authentic Wild West,* New York, Crown Publishers Inc., 1977. [H17]

Horn, Huston, *The Pioneers,* Alexandria, Time-Life Books, 1981. [H18]

Hornung, Chuck, "The Lynching of Gus Mentzer," *Real West,* April 1985. [H19]

Howes, Nick, "Johnny Fry of the Pony Express," *Real West,* March 1976. [H20]

Hughes, Stuart, ed., *The Frog Lake "Massacre,"* Toronto, McClelland & Stewart, 1976. [H21]

Hunt, Robert V. Jr., "Buttermilk Bill's Revenge," *Old West,* Fall 1992. [H22]

——, "Cicero C. Simms: Villain or Victim?," *Old West,* Fall 1994. [H23]

——, "A Colorado Predator," *True West,* August 1996. [H24]

——, "Grand Lake Fourth of July Massacre," *True West,* July 1994. [H25]

——, "High Country Assassins," *True West,* November 1995. [H26]

——, "Jack Smith: The General of Bull Hill," *True West,* September 1994. [H27]

——, "Mike Ryan," *True West,* October 1993. [H28]

——, "Not Fit To Die," *True West,* January 1992. [H29]

————, "Trinidad Terror," *Old West,* Fall 1995. [H30]

————, "Wyoming Sheriff Killer's Final Days," *True West,* April 1994. [H31]

Hutton, Harold, *Vigilante Days,* Chicago, Sage Books, The Swallow Press, 1978. [H32]

Hyde, Dayton O., *The Last Free Man,* New York, The Dial Press, 1973. [H33]

Jackson, Joseph Henry, *Bad Company,* Lincoln, University of Nebraska Press, 1977. [J1]

Jessen, Kenneth, *Colorado Gunsmoke,* Boulder, Pruett Publishing Company, 1986. [J2]

Johnson, Fred M., "The Hanging of George Woods," *True West,* December 1985. [J3]

Johnson, William Weber, *The Forty-niners,* Alexandria, Time-Life Books, 1980. [J4]

Kelly, Bill, "End of the Line for Jim Klein," *Real West,* January 1980. [K0]

————, "The Odyssey of Kid Lewis," *Real West,* March 1977. [K1]

Kilbane, Richard E., "Yakima Uprising," *True West,* November 1998. [K2]

Kildare, Maurice, "Doctor Grandma French," *Frontier Times,* July 1967 [K3].

King, Patrick, "Manen Clements Last of the Breed," *True West,* February 1995. [K4]

Klasner, Lily, *My Girlhood Among Outlaws,* Ed. Eve Ball, Tucson, The University of Arizona Press, 1988. [K5]

Kouris, Diana Allen, "The Lynching: Calamity in Brown's Park," *True West,* September 1995. [K6]

Krakel, Dean, *The Saga of Tom Horn,* Laramie, Powder River Publishers, 1954. [K7]

Kubista, Bob, "The Hanging of George Johnson," *Western Frontier,* May 1985. [K8]

Kutac, C., "The Last Days of Dennis Dilda," *Real West,* October 1985. [K9]

Lanza, Ruth Willett, "Aunt Clara Brown: The Black Angel of Central City," *True West,* April 1991. [L1]

————, "The Small But Deadly Espinosa Gang," *Wild West,* December, 1995. [L2]

Lapidus, Richard, "The Youngest Earp—Strange Events Surrounding the Death of Warren Earp," *WOLA Journal,* Vol. V, No. 1, 1995. [L3]

LaRocca, Linda, "Leadville's Evergreen Memories," *Old West,* Fall 1996. [L4]

Larson, E. Dixon and Al Ritter, "Gunfighters and Lawmen," *Wild West,* June 1996. [L5]

Lauer, Charles D., *Tales of Arizona Territory,* Phoenix, Golden West Publishers, 1990. [L6]

Laurance, B. F., "The Legendary Golden Chariot War," *Real West*, June 1987. [L7]

Le Comte, Edward S., *Dictionary of Last Words*, New York, Philosophical Library, 1955. [L8]

Lee, Joe, "My Wonderful Country," *Frontier Times*, March 1974. [L9]

Lee, Wayne C., *Bad Men & Bad Towns*, Caldwell, The Caxton Printers, Ltd., 1993. [L10]

Leiteritz, Gina M., "The School Board Murders," *Old West*, Spring 1997. [L11]

Lyman, George D., *The Saga of the Comstock Lode*, New York, Charles Scribner's Sons, 1949. [L12]

Macklin, William F., "Belles Behind Bars," *Old West*, Fall 1987. [M1]

Mallory, Burr H., "The Jest That Backfired," *Badman*, Fall 1972. [M2]

Martin, Douglas D., *Tombstone's Epitaph*, Albuquerque, The University of New Mexico, 1963. [M3]

Mather, R. E., "Cheating the Gallows," *True West*, January 1990. [M4]

——, "Gold Camp Mother Who Brought Down the Marshal," *True West*, November 1987. [M5]

——, "She Stood Up to the Vigilantes," *WOLA Journal*, Vol. II, No. 1, Spring-Summer, 1992. [M6]

Mather, R. E., and F. E. Boswell, *Gold Camp Desperadoes*, San Jose, History West Publishing, 1990. [M7]

——, *Vigilante Victims*, San Jose, History West Publishing Co., 1991. [M8]

Mathisen, Jean A., "His First Hanging," True *West*, April 1987. [M9]

——, "The Raid on the Jail," *True West*, April 1996. [M10]

Max, Matthew A., "The Prohibition War: Murder in Sioux City," *Wild West*, October 1998. [M11]

McCarty, John L., *Maverick Town*, Norman, University of Oklahoma Press, 1988. [M12]

McInnes, Elmer D., "Bloody Night in a Boise Bagnio," *WOLA Journal*, Vol. I, No. 3, Spring 1992. [M13]

——, "Con Murphy: A Daisy of an Outlaw," *True West*, December 1999. [M14]

——, "Dave Mullen—A Desperate Man," *NOLA Quarterly*, Vol. XVII, No. 2, April–June 1993. [M15]

——, "Jack O'Neil—Man On The Road To Brimstone," *NOLA Quarterly*, Vol. XVII, No. 4, Oct.–Dec. 1993. [M16]

——, "Pete Bannigan—A Bad Man From Brainerd," *NOLA Quarterly*, Vol. XIX, No. 3, July–Sept. 1995. [M17]

——, "The Terrible McWaters: Part Two," *True West*, February 1998. [M18]

————, "Wyatt Earp's Coeur D'Alene Comrade," *Old West*, Spring 1996. [M19]

McKanna, Bud, "Gallows and Gunfights in Old San Diego," *True West* June 1986. [M20]

McKelvie, B. A., *Tales of Conflict*, Surrey, Heritage House Publishing Co., 1985. [M21]

McMillan, Mark, "Lucky Bill Gets the Noose," *Badman*, Vol. 1, No. 1, 1971. [M22]

Meier, Gary, "The Mystery of Santa Clara Valley," *True West*, October 1989. [M23]

Meketa, Jacqueline, "She Died To Save Others," *Real West*, January 1988. [M24]

Metz, Leon Claire, *Dallas Stoudenmire El Paso Marshal*, Norman, University of Oklahoma Press, 1993. [M25]

————, "An Incident at Christmas," *NOLA Quarterly*, Vol. XIV, No. 1, 1990. [M26]

————, *John Selman, Gunfighter*, Norman, University of Oklahoma Press, 1980. [M27]

————, *John Wesley Hardin*, El Paso, Mangan Books, 1996. [M28]

————, *Pat Garrett*, Norman, University of Oklahoma Press, 1987. [M29]

Meyers, John Meyers, *The Last Chance*, Lincoln, University of Nebraska Press, 1973. [M30]

Michno, Greg, "Lakota Noon at the Greasy Grass," *Wild West*, June 1996. [M31]

Miller, Don, "Cargoes of Death," *True West*, October 1980. [M32]

Nelson, Andre, "The Last Sheepman-Cattleman War," *True West*, May 1988. [N1]

Nelson, Christopher, "Last Voyage of The Tonquin," *Wild West*, December 1992. [N2]

Nevin, David, *The Mexican War*, Alexandria, Time-Life Books, 1979. [N3]

————, *The Soldiers*, Alexandria, Time-Life Books, 1981. [N4]

————, *The Texans*, Alexandria, Time-Life Books, 1975. [N5]

Newman, Peter C., *Company of Adventurers*, Vol. I, Markham, Viking Penguin Books, 1985. [N6]

Niderost, Eric, "The Battle of the Washita," *Wild West*, October 1998. [N7]

Nielson, Carole, "Tunnel 13 Holdup," *Wild West*, June 1994. [N8]

Nolan, Frederick, *Bad Blood*, Stillwater, Barbed Wire Press, 1994. [N9]

————, "Boss Rustler," Part I, *True West*, September 1996. [N10]

O'Dell, Roy, "Arizona's Flour-Sack Bandit," *True West*, January 1989. [O1]

————, "Arizona's Forgotten Escape Artist," *Old West*, Fall 1990. [O2]

————, "Milton Sharp, Scourge of Wells, Fargo, *NOLA Quarterly,* Vol. XXIII, No. 3, July–Sept. 1999. [O3]

————, "Timbuctoo Terror," *The Brand Book,* London, The English Westerners' Society, 1988-89. [O4]

O'Dell, Roy, and Barbara Hegne, "Dangerous Men: 'Bloody Knife' and the 'Pigeon-Toed Kid' ," *True West,* September 1995. [O5]

O'Donnell, Jeff, "The Only Legal Hanging In Custer County," *Real West,* October 1988. [O6]

O'Neal, Bill, *The Arizona Rangers,* Austin, Eakin Press, 1987. [O7]

————, *Cattlemen vs Sheepherders,* Austin, Eakin Press, 1989. [O8]

————, *Encyclopedia of Western Gunfighters,* Norman, University of Oklahoma Press, 1979. [O9]

————, *Fighting Men of the Indian Wars,* Stillwater, Barbed Wire Press, 1991. [O10]

————, *Henry Brown, The Outlaw Marshal,* College Station, Creative Publishing Company, 1980. [O11]

————, "Temple Houston and Jack Love vs. Ed and John Jennings," *True West,* July 1992. [O12]

————, "The Woodpeckers vs. the Jaybirds," *True West,* September 1993. [O13]

Outlaws & Lawmen of Western Canada, Vol. Two, Surrey, Heritage House Publishing Co., 1983. [O14]

Outlaws & Lawmen of Western Canada, Vol. Three, Surrey, Heritage House Publishing Co., 1987. [O15]

Parsons, Chuck and Marjorie, *Bowen and Hardin,* College Station, Creative Publishing Company, 1991. [P1]

Patterson, T. W., *Outlaws of Western Canada,* Langley, Mr. Paperback, 1982. [P2]

Perkins, Randy, "The Lynching of Danny Arata," *True West,* July 1988. [P3]

Peters, James Stevens, "The Strangulation of Damian Romero," *Old West,* Summer 1983. [P4]

Pioche Daily Record, August 2, 1873. [P5]

Price, Will, "Lonesome Charley," *True West,* June 1961. [P6]

Rasch, Philip J., "The Brief Careers of Billy Grounds and Zwing Hunt," *Real West,* February 1985. [R1]

————, "Fleming 'Jim' Parker, Arizona Desperado," *NOLA Quarterly,* Vol. VII, No. 1, Spring 1982. [R2]

————, "One Killed, One Wounded," *NOLA Quarterly,* Vol. IV, No. 2, Autumn 1978. [R3]

————, "'Six Shooter' and 'Three Shooter' Smith," *NOLA Quarterly,* Vol. IX, No. 4, Spring 1985. [R4]

Reese, John Walter and Lillian Estelle Reese, ed., *Flaming Feuds of Colorado County,* Salado, The Anson Jones Press, 1962. [R5]

Reidhead, S. J., "Kit Carson: American Hero," *Wild West,* April 1999. [R6]

Reynolds, William D., "Frank Baker: Forgotten Gunman of the Lincoln County War," *NOLA Quarterly,* Vol. XV, No. 3, July–Sept. 1991. [R7]

Rezatto, Helen, *Mount Moriah,* Aberdeen, North Plains Press, 1987. [R8]

———, "Patrick Casey's Spectacular Suicide," *True West,* August 1983. [R9]

Richards, Walter L., "Shootout at Stoneville," *True West,* July 1992. [R10]

Riotte, Louise, "Marshal Braziel and Bud Ballew," *Frontier Times,* November 1980. [R11]

Robbins, Peggy, "King of the Keelboatmen," *Wild West,* December 1992. [R12]

Roberts, Gary L., "From Tin Star to Hanging Tree: The Short Career and Violent Times of Billy Brooks," *The Prairie Scout,* Vol. Three, Abilene, The Kansas Corral of the Westerners, Inc., 1975. [R13]

Robinson, Charles M. III, "Buffalo Chips," *True West,* October 1994. [R14]

———, "Fort Fetterman, Rip-roaring Cowtown," *Old West,* Winter 1994. [R15]

———, "Kicking Bird: Kiowa Martyr for Peace," *True West,* January 1993. [R16]Roebuck, Field, "The True Story of The Brazos Indian Reserve Skirmish," *Old West,* Spring 1988. [R17]

Rogers, Lisa Waller, "The Hanging of Bob Augustine," *True West,* August 1997. [R18]

Rosa, Joseph G., "'Little Dave's' Last Fight: What Really Happened When Wild Bill Hickok and Davis K. Tutt Shot It Out At Springfield, Missouri," *NOLA Quarterly,* Vol. XX, No. 4, Oct.–Dec. 1996. [R19]

———, *They Called Him Wild Bill,* Norman, University of Oklahoma Press, 1982. [R20]

Rose, Sammie and Pat Wood, "Gunfighters and Lawmen," *Wild West,* April 1997. [R21]

Sampson, Joanna, "Outgunned in Meeker," *True West,* May 1995. [S1]

Samuelson, Nancy B., "Flora Quick aka Mrs. Mundis aka Tom King aka China Dot," *NOLA Quarterly,* Vol. XX, No. 4, Oct.–Dec. 1996. [S2]

Schoenberger, Dale T., *End of Custer,* Surrey, Hancock House Publishers Ltd., 1995. [S3]

Scott, David, and Roy Bird, "A Cavalry Campaign Gone Wrong," *Real West,* December 1985. [S4]

Secrest, William B., *Dangerous Trails: Five Desperadoes of the Old West Coast,* Stillwater, Barbed Wire Press, 1995. [S5]

———, "Dead Men and Desperadoes," *True West,* May 1989. [S6]

————, "The Man Who Escaped," Part II, *True West*, December 1996. [S7]

Selcer, Richard F., *Hell's Half Acre*, Fort Worth, Texas Christian University Press, 1991. [S8]

Sellers, Grace, "Revenge By Fire," *Frontier Times*, July 1972. [S9]

Severs, Vesta-Nadine, "Wild Lewis Boys: Terrors of Newton County," *True West*, October 1999. [S10]

Shirley, Glenn, *The Fighting Marlows*, Fort Worth, Texas Christian University Press, 1994. [S11]

————, *Guardian of the Law*, Austin, Eakin Press, 1988. [S12]

————, *Heck Thomas, Frontier Marshal*, Norman, University of Oklahoma Press, 1981. [S13]

————, "The Homicide, The Healer, and the Hangman," *Old West*, Winter 1995. [S14]

————, "The Honorable Death of Silan Lewis," *True West*, June 1991. [S15]

————, *Law West of Fort Smith*, Lincoln, Bison Books, University of Nebraska Press, 1969. [S16]

————, *Marauders of the Indian Nations*, Barbed Wire Press, 1994. [S17]

————, "A Mean Hombre," *True West*, February 1989. [S18]

————, *Shotgun For Hire*, Norman, University of Oklahoma Press, 1980. [S19]

————, *West of Hell's Fringe*, Norman, University of Oklahoma Press, 1978. [S20]

Shulsinger, Stephanie Cooper, "The Unforgettable Custers," *Real West*, September 1975. [S21]

Simpson, Audrey, "Hermit's Peak Legend," *Old West*, Spring 1988. [S22]

Simpson, John J., "Jack Sully—King of the Dakota Rustlers," *WOLA Journal*, Vol. IV, No. 1, Spring 1994. [S23]

Smith, Robert Barr, "Shootout at Ingalls," *Wild West*, October 1992. [S24]

————, "Texas John's Odyssey," *Wild West*, December 1993. [S25]

Smith, Robert Benjamin, "Apache Captives' Ordeal," *Wild West*, June 1993. [S26]

————, "Audacious Outlaw Tom Bell," *Wild West*, February 1994 [S27].

————, "Cornered Killer," *Wild West*, December 1992. [S28]

Snell, Joseph W., "Double Shooting in Hays," *Old West*, Spring 1972. [S29]

Sonnichsen, C. L., *I'll Die Before I'll Run*, New York, The Devin-Adair Company, 1962. [S30]

————, *Ten Texas Feuds*, Albuquerque, University of New Mexico Press, 1971. [S31]

Speer, Lonnie R., "On the Trail of the Barefoot Outlaws," *True West*, July 1989. [S32]

Staniford, Mike, "Tom Jordan, Cherokee Outlaw," *True West*, November 1985. [S33]

Stano, Mary G., "The Last Battle of James Malone," *True West*, September 1994. [S34]

Steele, Phillip, *The Last Cherokee Warriors*, Gretna, Pelican Publishing Company, 1974. [S35]

———, "The Shannon-Fisher War," *Old West*, Fall 1985. [S36]

———, "The Tragic Death of Deputy U.S. Marshal Frank Dalton," *NOLA Quarterly*, Vol. XVI, No. 4, Oct.–Dec. 1992. [S37]

Stonechild, Blair and Bill Waiser, *Loyal till Death*, Calgary, Fifth House Ltd., 1997. [S38]

Sullivan, Sergeant W. J. L., *Twelve Years in the Saddle*, New York, Buffalo Head Press, 1966. [S39]

Swanson, Budington, "They Cleaned Up The West," *True West*, December 1988. [S40]

Taylor, Paul, "T. S. Harris, Hard Luck Journalist," *Old West*, Winter 1985. [T0]

Tefertiller, Casey, *Wyatt Earp*, New York, John Wiley & Sons, Inc., 1997. [T1]

Thompson, George A., "Only An Indian," *Real West*, December 1986. [T2]

Thompson, Jerry, "Gunfight At The NH Corral," *Wild West*, April 1998. [T3]

Thorp, Raymond W. and William B. Secrest, "Colter's Boone," *Old West*, Summer 1966. [T4]

———, "The Return of Jim McKinney," *True West*, February 1963. [T5]

Time-Life Books, *The Gamblers*, Alexandria, Virginia, 1980. [T6]

———, *The Spanish West*, Alexandria, Virginia, 1979. [T7]

Trenerry, Walter N., *Murder in Minnesota*, St. Paul, Minnesota Historical Society, 1962. [T8]

Torrez, Robert J., "The Man Who Was Hanged Twice," *True West*, November 1989. [T9]

Turner, Alford E., "The Clantons of Apache County," *Real West*, March 1979. [T10]

Twain, Mark, *The Autobiography of Mark Twain*, New York, Harper & Brothers, 1959. [T11]

Underwood, Larry, "George Drouillard, Frontier Scout," *True West*, November 1987. [U1]

———, "Golden Justice," *True West*, December 1990. [U2]

———, "Murder or Duty," *True West*, January 1997. [U3]

———, "Poker and Poolcues," *True West*, February 1997. [U4]

———, "The Wild and Wooly West Makes A Widow," *Old West*, Spring 1996. [U5]

Utley, Robert M., *Billy the Kid,* Lincoln, University of Nebraska Press, 1989. [U6]

——, *The Lance and the Shield,* New York, Henry Holt and Company, 1993. [U7]

Van Raalte, Ronald C., "He Was the Thorn of Rosebud," *WOLA The Journal,* Vol. V, No. 2., 1996. [V1]

Varnell, Jeanne, "Musgrove's Last Jailbreak," *True West,* August, 1994. [V2]

Vestal, Stanley, *Sitting Bull,* Norman, University of Oklahoma Press, 1957. [V3]

Von Schweinitz, Helga, "Hermann Ehrenberg—Fighting for Texas," *True West,* April 1986. [V4]

Wallace, Alice Wright, "A man Who Knew Guns," *Frontier Times,* May 1968. [W1]

Warren, D. E., "The Story of 'Two Others'," *Frontier Times,* December 1964. [W2]

Webb, Walter Prescott, "McNelly's Rangers," *True West,* August 1983. [W3]

Webster, M. L., "Storm in the Wind," *Wild West,* August 1993. [W4]

Weekes, Mary, *The Last Buffalo Hunter,* Saskatoon, Fifth House Publishers, 1994. [W5]

Welch, Julia Conway, *The Magruder Murders,* Eagle Point, Julia Conway Welch, 1991. [W6]

White, Marian B., "A Great Explorer's Final Hours," *Frontier Times,* May 1980. [W7]

Williams, Gary, "Hangings in Old Spokane," *Western Frontier,* November 1982. [W8]

Williams, Richard L., *The Loggers,* Alexandria, Time-Life Books, Inc., 1979. [W9]

Wiltsey, Norman B., "Last of the Hide Hunters," *True West,* October 1957. [W10]

Wittels, Sylvia, "Doc's Disease," *True West,* April 1997. [W11]

Wolfe, George D., "Hanging of 38 Sioux," *True West,* December 1956. [W12]

Woodcock, George, *Gabriel Dumont,* Edmonton, Hurtig Publishers, 1975. [W13]

Wright, Chris J., "Fields of Fire," *True West,* August 1995. [W14]

Yost, Nellie Snyder, *Buffalo Bill,* Chicago, The Swallow Press, 1979. [Y1]

Zehnder, Chuck, "Gunfighters & Lawmen," *Wild West,* June 1991. [Z1]

INDEX

[Bracketed numbers] refer to sources: See bibliography

—C—

—F—

Faddiman (Bartender) [F6], 169
Fafard, Leon Adelard (Priest) [H21], 186
Farr, Edward J. (Sheriff) [B26], 141
Farris, Sam (Deputy) [S20], 155
Ferguson, Annie (Prostitute) [C2], 171
Fielder, Dan (Homesteader) [F8], 16
Fields, Will (Indian Police) [B32], 139
Fink, Mike (Boatman) [R12], 3
Fisher, Jarrett (Outlaw) [S36], 110
Fisher, John King (Gunman) [H15], 132
Floyd, Charles (Sergeant) [F6], 1
Fooy, Sam (Murderer) [S16], 64
Ford, Robert (Saloon Owner) [D9], 209
Four Bears (Mandan Warrior) [M32], 30
Fox, John (First Officer) [N2], 187
Fream, Dave (Cowboy) [C4], 15
Fredericks, William (Murderer) [E2], 87
Free, Mickey (Murderer) [C17], 221
French, Emma (Pioneer) [K3], 45
French, John (Captain, Canadian Army) [H8], 187
Friar, Art (Horse Thief) [O9], 74
Frost, Ben (Rancher) [B12], 44
Frost, Mart (Rancher) [B12], 20
Funk, Ed S. (Hired Gun) [H7], 133

—G—

Gallagher, Bill (Outlaw) [S25], 111
Gallagher, Jack (Outlaw), 49
Gantz, Jacob (Immigrant) [J2], 42
Garland, William A. (Hop Fiend) [S2], 218
Garnier, Baptiste "Little Bat" (Guide/Scout) [B14], 63
Garrett, Patrick (Former Lawman) [M29], 133
Garten, Theodore (Gambler) [L9], 26
Garvey, Jim (Sheriff) [O13], 181

Gay, William "Bill" (Murderer) [L5], 88
Gibson, Mary (Saloon Owner) [S5], 169
Goldsby, Crawford "Cherokee Bill" (Murderer) [S17], 65
Goodbread, Joseph (Murder Victim) [S31], 12
Gordon, James (Murderer) [D20], 77
Gordon, Kirk (Guide) [B27], 60
Gowanlock, John (Millwright) [H21], 186
Grant, Joe (Gunfighter) [U6], 132
Graydon, James "Paddy" (Captain) [B27], 57
Greathouse "Whiskey Jim" (Rustler) [B26], 112
Greer, W. W. "Duck Man" [H9], 157
Grimes, Ellis (Deputy Sheriff) [A5], 138

—H—

Haddock, George Channing (Minister) [M11], 181
Hafen, Wilford (Pioneer Child) [H0], 45
Halderman, Thomas (Rustler) [B7], 165
Halderman, William (Rustler) [B7], 165
Hale, John (Rancher) [M25], 158
Hamilton, Louis Malone (Captain) [O10], 61
Hardin, John Wesley (Gunfighter) [M28], 159
Hare, Alexander (Outlaw) [O14], 80
Harmison, Frank (Mob Member) [S11], 122
Harper, Thomas (Cowboy) [T1], 162
Harrington, Dan (Bootlegger) [B9], 144
Harris, Jack (Theater Owner) [C18], 20
Harris, James M. (Settler) [E5], 43

Parker, Fleming "Jim" (Outlaw)
[D19/R2], 201

Parnell, Tom (Gunfight Loser) [A4], 24

Parrott, "Big Nose" George (Outlaw)
[E9], 103

Pascale (Kootenais Indian) [E10], 36

Patterson, Ferd (Gambler) [D9], 54

Patterson, W. P. (Cattleman) [O9], 145

Phillips, William (Murder Victim)
[W6], 42

Picariello, Emilio (Bootlegger) [O15],
202

Pierson, George (Saloon Owner)
[D11], 216

Pinckney, Tom (Shooting Victim)
[S31], 182

Pinkham, Sumner "Old Pink"
(Deputy U.S. Marshal) [D9], 137

Pitts, Charlie (Outlaw) [B17], 71

Plummer, Henry (Sheriff) [M8], 48

Policy Bob (Gambler) [D9], 56

Porter, Benjamin C. (Actor) [R3], 173

Potee, Bob (Gambler) [D9], 54

Power, Ola May (Cook) [F0], 178

Power, T. J. "Jeff" (Goldminer) [F0],
178

Proctor, Zeke (Former Lawman)
[S35], 224

Pryde, John E. (Lumbercamp Cook)
[T8], 56

Puebla, Librado (Convict) [S19], 115

Pushmataha (Choctaw Chief) [H4], 29

—Q—

Qualchan (Yakima Warrior) [B5], 31

Quick, Flora "Tom King" (Outlaw)
[S2], 218

Quinn, Thomas Trueman (Indian
Agent) [H21], 185

—R—

Rader, William (Deputy) [L5], 155

Ramirez, Rodriguez (Bandit Leader)
[G4], 75

"Rattlesnake Dick." *See* Barter,
Richard A.

Ray, Ed (Deputy) [M6], 48

Red Jacket (Seneca Chief) [A0], 29-
30

Redd, William (Captain) [C18], 12

Redman, William (Deputy) [H25],
181

Reese, Samuel Houston (Rancher)
[R5], 23

Renfro, Lee (Outlaw) [T10], 146

Renton, David (Outlaw) [M7], 77

Reynolds, "Lonesome" Charley
(Scout) [P6], 68

Richardson, Levi (Freighter) [D3],
131

Riddle, George (Murder Victim)
[H12], 23

Riel, Louis David (Metis Leader)
[H8], 188-189

Rivet, Antoine (Voyageur) [M21], 3

Roberts, Andrew L. "Buckshot" [O9],
150

Roe, William M. (Murderer) [C2], 89

Roesch, Andreas (Murderer) [T8], 78

Rogers, Bob (Outlaw) [S16], 207

Rohn, Samuel (Shooting Victim)
[M20], 113

Romain, James (Outlaw) [W6], 77

Romero, Damian (Murderer) [P4], 82

Romero, Deonicio (Outlaw) [H30], 88

Rooke, Sarah J. "Sally" (Telephone
Operator) [M24], 177

Ross, Tom (Ranch Foreman) [D5], 215

Rover, J. W. (Miner) [B2], 199-200

Rowland, John (Factor) [W5], 4

Royer, Charles W. (Sheriff) [H25],
180-181

Rucker, Oliver (Gambler) [D9], 53

Ryan, Mike (Con Man) [H28], 157

—S—

Sager, Henry (Pioneer) [M8], 39

Satank (Kiowa Chief) [F1], 34

Schwartz, Al (Rancher), 121

—T—

Townsend, Samuel C. (Police Officer) [U5], 139

Tracy, J. A. (Mine Agent) [O7], 219

Travis, William Barret (Lieutenant-Colonel) [F1], 8

Tunstall, John Henry (Rancher) [U6], 149

Tutt, Davis K. (Gambler) [R19], 54

Tuttle, Harry (Outlaw) [R10], 106

Two Face (Oglala Chief) [S4], 33

—U—

Urieta, Leandro (Murderer) [N10], 130

Ussher, John (Constable) [O14], 138

—V—

Van Orsdel, William Wesley (Circuit Rider) [F9], 225

Vasquez, Tiburcio (Outlaw) [C12], 70

Vaughan (Raft Captain) [H1], 40

Vedder, John (Gambler) [M5], 127

—W—

Wade, John (Horse Thief) [H32], 105

Wagner, Henry "The Flying Dutchman" (Outlaw) [H3], 92

Wagner, "Dutch" John [M8], 49

Waker, Billy (Vigilante) [H7], 85-86

Walker, Dave (Vigilante) [H7], 84

Walker, Samuel Hamilton (Captain) [G8], 28

Wall, S. H. (Sheepman) [H24], 43

Walters, J. P. (Murderer) [M10], 122

Wandering Spirit (Cree War Chief) [H21], 190

Washakie (Shoshoni Chief) [C14], 37

Watson, Stephen (Second Lieutenant) [F5], 58

Watson, William (Colonel) [N3], 28

Webb, Charley (Deputy Sheriff) [A5], 137

Webb, Jim (Fugitive) [B32], 145

Weber, E. P. (County Commissioner) [H25], 180

Webster, Jim (Fugitive) [O4], 128

Welsh, Peter (Private) [S29], 61

Westaway, Harry (Canadian Mountie) [O14], 142

Wheeler, Ben (Outlaw) [O11], 104

White Antelope (Cheyenne Chief), 33

White Dog (Sioux Warrior) [W12], 32

White, Jonathan "Buffalo Chips" (Scout) [R14], 62

Whitney, Chauncey (Sheriff) [O9], 137

Whittington, William (Murderer) [S16], 65

Wilkinson, Burt (Outlaw) [B11], 105

Wilkinson, Melville Cary (Major) [W4], 63

Williams (Settler) [G7], 16

Williams, Edgar (Town Marshal) [V1], 141

Williams, James H. (Texas Ranger) [B6], 167

Williamson, Tim (Ranch Foreman) [S31], 17

Williscroft, John (Shooting Victim) [H21], 186

Willoughby, William (Gunfight Loser) [C15], 128

Wilson, Billie (Cowboy) [D8], 15

Wilson, Charles W. "Texas Charley" (Troublemaker) [J2], 112

Wilson, Floyd (Lawman) [O9], 140

Wilson, Mark (Theater Owner) [O9], 171

Wilson, Tom "Doc" (Settler) [F1], 42

Wilson, William (Cowboy) [K5], 79

Wilson, William J. (Cattle Baron) [H22], 25

Winney, DeWitt (Sergeant) [S3], 69

Wiseman, Loren (Pioneer Child) [C3], 42

Wohrle, John (Ex-Deputy Sheriff) [B25], 17

Wong Bock Sing (Launderer) [D11], 177

Wood, Andrew (Outlaw) [S7], 96

Woodruff, Sam (Murderer) [U2], 102